雙雙中文教材 (18)
Chinese Language and Culture Course

中國古代哲學 Ancient Chinese Philosophy

王雙雙 編著

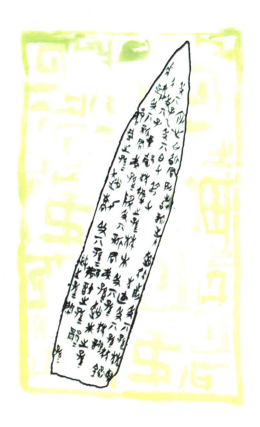

北京大學出版社
PEKING UNIVERSITY PRESS

圖書在版編目（CIP）數據

中國古代哲學：繁體版／（美）王雙雙編著．—北京：北京大學出版社，2009.1
（雙雙中文教材18）
ISBN 978-7-301-14414-5

Ⅰ.中… Ⅱ.王… Ⅲ.①漢語－對外漢語教學－教材 ②哲學史－中國－古代 Ⅳ.H195.4

中國版本圖書館CIP數據核字（2008）第168378號

書　　　　名：	中國古代哲學
著作責任者：	王雙雙 編著
英 文 翻 譯：	陶友蘭
插　　　　圖：	王金秦
責 任 編 輯：	孫　嫻
標 準 書 號：	ISBN 978-7-301-14414-5/H・2099
出 版 發 行：	北京大學出版社
地　　　　址：	北京市海淀區成府路205號　100871
網　　　　址：	http://www.pup.cn
電　　　　話：	郵購部 62752015　發行部 62750672　編輯部 62752028　出版部 62754962
電子信箱：	zpup@pup.pku.edu.cn
印　刷　者：	北京大學印刷廠
經　銷　者：	新華書店
	889毫米×1194毫米　16開本　8.5印張　119千字
	2009年1月第1版　2009年1月第1次印刷
定　　　　價：	90.00元（含課本、練習冊和CD-ROM一張）

未經許可，不得以任何方式複製或抄襲本書之部分或全部內容。
版權所有，侵權必究
舉報電話：010-62752024
電子信箱：fd@pup.pku.edu.cn

前 言

《雙雙中文教材》是一套專門為海外青少年編寫的中文課本，是我在美國八年的中文教學實踐基礎上編寫成的。在介紹這套教材之前，請讀一首小詩：

> 一雙神奇的手，
> 推開一扇窗。
> 一條神奇的路，
> 通向燦爛的中華文化。
>
> 鮑凱文　鮑維江
> 1998年

鮑維江和鮑凱文姐弟倆是美國生美國長的孩子，也是我的學生。1998年冬，他們送給我的新年賀卡上的小詩，深深地打動了我的心。我把這首詩看成我文化教學的"回聲"。我要傳達給海外每位中文老師：我教給他們（學生）中國文化，他們思考了、接受了、回應了。這條路走通了！

語言是交際的工具，更是一種文化和一種生活方式，所以學習中文也就離不開中華文化的學習。漢字是一種古老的象形文字，她從遠古走來，帶有大量的文化信息，但學起來並不容易。使學生增強興趣、減小難度，走出苦學漢字的怪圈，走進領悟中華文化的花園，是我編寫這套教材的初衷。

學生不論大小，天生都有求知的慾望，都有欣賞文化美的追求。中華文化本身是魅力十足的。把這宏大而玄妙的文化，深入淺出地，有聲有色地介紹出來，讓這迷人的文化如涓涓細流，一點一滴地滲入學生們的心田，使學生們逐步體味中國文化，是我編寫這套教材的目的。

為此我將漢字的學習放入文化介紹的流程之中同步進行，讓同學們在學中國地理的同時，學習漢字；在學中國歷史的同時，學習漢字；在學中國哲學的同時，學習漢字；在學中國科普文選的同時，學習漢字……

這樣的一種中文學習，知識性強，趣味性強；老師易教，學生易學。當學生們合上書本時，他們的眼前是中國的大好河山，是中國五千年的歷史和妙不可言的哲學思維，是奔騰的現代中國……

總之，他們瞭解了中華文化，就會探索這片土地，熱愛這片土地，就會與中國結下情緣。

最後我要衷心地感謝所有熱情支持和幫助我編寫教材的老師、家長、學生、朋友和家人，特別是老同學唐玲教授、何茜老師、我姐姐王欣欣編審及我女兒Uta Guo年復一年的鼎力相助。可以說這套教材是大家努力的結果。

王雙雙

說　明

　　《雙雙中文教材》是一套專門為海外學生編寫的中文教材。它是由美國加州王雙雙老師和中國專家學者共同努力，在海外多年的實踐中編寫出來的。全書共20冊，識字量2500個，包括了從識字、拼音、句型、短文的學習，到初步的較系統的中國文化的學習。教材大體介紹了中國地理、歷史、哲學等方面的豐富內容，突出了中國文化的魅力。課本知識面廣，趣味性強，深入淺出，易教易學。

　　這套教材體系完整、構架靈活、使用面廣。學生可以從零起點開始，一直學完全部課程20冊；也可以將後11冊（10～20冊）的九個文化專題和第五冊（漢語拼音）單獨使用，這樣便於開設中國哲學、地理、歷史等專門課程以及假期班、短期中國文化班、拼音速成班的高中和大學使用，符合了美國AP中文課程的目標和基本要求。

　　這本《中國古代哲學》是《雙雙中文教材》的第十八冊，由王雙雙在陳戰國先生（北京社會科學院哲學所所長）的指導和幫助下，經過多年的努力，在海外中文教學實踐的基礎上編寫而成。全書以簡單的語言，將中國先秦哲學倫理思想作了概括介紹。通過對本書的學習，學生將會基本瞭解中國古代儒、道兩家的思想，不僅能提高中文水平，也能提高思辨能力，從而可以在思想的層面上領略中華文化的精妙之處。

　　這裏還要特別鳴謝曹儒伯先生在英文翻譯上給予的幫助。

編者

課程設置

一年級	中文課本（第一冊）	中文課本（第二冊）	中文課本（第三冊）
二年級	中文課本（第四冊）	中文課本（第五冊）	中文課本（第六冊）
三年級	中文課本（第七冊）	中文課本（第八冊）	中文課本（第九冊）
四年級	中國成語故事	中國地理常識	
五年級	中國古代故事	中國神話傳說	
六年級	中國古代科學技術	中國文學欣賞	
七年級	中國詩歌欣賞	中文科普閱讀	
八年級	中國古代哲學	中國歷史（上）	
九年級	中國歷史（下）	小說閱讀，中文SAT II	
十年級	中文SAT II（強化班）	小說閱讀，中文SAT II 考試	

目　錄

第一課　　　孔子的思想 …………………… 1

第二課　　　孟子的思想 …………………… 11

第三課　　　荀子的思想 …………………… 20

第四課　　　墨子的思想 …………………… 29

第五課　　　老子的思想 …………………… 38

第六課　　　莊子的思想 …………………… 48

第七課　　　孫子的思想 …………………… 58

第八課　　《易經》的思想 …………………… 68

生字表 ………………………………………… 76

生詞表 ………………………………………… 78

第一課

孔子的思想

孔子（前551—前479）是中國偉大的思想家、教育家。他與古希臘的蘇格拉底、印度的釋迦牟尼(jiā móu)生活在同一時代，是中國的聖人。他的思想對於中國和世界都有很大的影響。他創立了儒家學派。

孔子一生都在努力教導人們如何做人，如何做有道德的人。他告訴人們，做一個道德高尚的人必須做到以下幾點：

一、"愛人"。有一個學生問孔子什麼是"仁"？他解釋說："愛人。""仁"指最高尚的道德品質，也指有高尚道德品質的人。孔子認為，人最根本、最高尚的品質就是愛人。一個人只有能夠愛別人，纔是一個有道德的人。

孔子像

愛人要真誠，而不能虛情假意。愛人首先是愛自己的父母、愛自己的兄弟姐妹、愛自己的朋友，因為這些人與你天天生活在一起，和你最有感情。從自己的親人愛起，從自己身邊的人愛起，一直到愛所有的人，愛所有的物，愛整個宇宙。

真誠地愛自己的親人容易，真誠地愛一切人、一切物很難。一個人總有他喜歡的人，也有他不喜歡的人；總有他喜歡的物，也有他不喜歡的物。要想做到愛一切人和一切物，就必須有很高的精神境界，把整個世界看成是一個大家庭。中國宋朝有一個叫張載的人說過，天是父親，地是母親，所有的人都是我的兄弟姐妹，所有的物都是我的同類。當時還有一個叫程顥（hào）的人說，整個宇宙是一個大生命，宇宙間的一切東西都是血肉相連的，這種血肉相連的關係就是"仁"，割斷了這種關係就是"不仁"。一個人只有把自己放入整個宇宙之中，只有像愛自己的生命一樣地去愛宇宙中的一切，纔是一個有最高道德品質的人。他們的這些思想都是從孔子的思想中發展出來的。

二、"忠恕"。"忠"是盡心盡力地幫助別人，"恕"是對別人要寬容。孔子說"己欲立而立人，己欲達而達人"，"己所不欲，勿施於人"。人都希望得到幸福、快樂和事業上的成功，都不希望遭到不幸、痛苦和失敗。因此，一個有道德的人就應該幫助別人得到幸福、快樂和成功，幫助別人免遭不幸、痛苦和失敗。自己希望得到的，應該幫助別人也得到；自己不願意遇到的情況，也應該幫助別人不要遇到；希望別人怎麼對自己，自己也應該怎麼去對別人。這一做人的原則，叫做"忠恕之道"。

三、"克己復禮"。"克己"就是克制自己的私慾，約束自己的行為；"復禮"就是遵守各種社會規範。為了使社會穩定，人們定出了許多規範，用來約束人們的行為。一個有道德的人，就要自覺地遵守各種社會規範，做對社會有益的事，不要破壞社會秩序。

孔子教人怎麼做人的思想很豐富，以上三點是最重要的。人們只要努力按照這三點去做，就一定能夠成為一個道德高尚的人。

王金泰 畫

中國古代哲學

生詞

jiào yù 教育	education		kuānróng 寬容	tolerant
xī là 希臘	Greek		shī 施	carry out; do
rú jiā 儒家	Confucianism		shì yè 事業	career
xué pài 學派	school of thought		kè zhì 克制	restraint
dào dé 道德	morality		yuē shù 約束	restrict
gāo shàng 高尚	noble		xíng wéi 行為	behaviour
jiě shì 解釋	explain		zūn shǒu 遵守	comply with; observe
gǎn qíng 感情	emotion		guī fàn 規範	standards and norms
jīng shén jìng jiè 精神境界	spiritual state; mental outlook		wěn dìng 穩定	stable
gē duàn 割斷	cut off; sever		zhì xù 秩序	order
zhōng shù 忠恕	loyalty and forbearance			

聽寫

感情　道德　教育　遵守　穩定　解釋　行為　高尚

秩序　割斷　*施　忠恕

注：*以後的字詞為選做題，後同。

比一比

創 { 創造 / 創立　　克 { 克制 / 克服　　派 { 學派 / 派人　　尚 { 高尚 / 和尚

束 { 約束 / 結束　　境 { 境界 / 環境　　序 { 秩序 / 順序　　範 { 規範 / 範圍

詞語運用

遵守　　尊敬

要遵守交通規則，不要闖紅燈。

我們要尊敬老人。

品質

熱心幫助別人是一種好品質。

哥哥不僅學習好，品質也好。

近義詞

有益——有利

反義詞

真誠——虛偽　　　　有益——有害

根據課文回答問題

1. 孔子是什麼時期的人？

2. 孔子創立了什麼學派？

3. 請解釋孔子"仁"、"忠"、"恕"的思想。

4. 請解釋孔子的"愛人"的思想和"忠恕之道"。

5. 什麼是"己欲立而立人，己欲達而達人"，"己所不欲，勿施於人"？

詞語解釋

有益——有好處；有幫助。

真誠——真心實意，沒有一點虛假。

創立——初次建立。

免遭——避免遇到。

虛情假意——對人的感情不是真心的，而是假裝出來的。

閱讀

孔子簡介

孔子,名丘,字仲尼,春秋時期魯國人,著名的教育家、思想家,儒家學派的創始人。孔子曾代理魯國宰相,後周遊列國,推行自己的政治主張,但都沒有成功。他晚年整理古代文化典籍,編訂了"六經"[①]等書,對中國文化發展貢獻極大。

孔子好學

孔子從小十分好學,學習上有了問題就向人請教,一定要弄明白。孔子學習不僅僅要學會,還要做到精益求精。

有一次他跟老師學琴。一支曲子學了十幾天,老師很滿意地說:"彈得不錯,可以學新曲子了。"孔子卻不滿意,說:"曲子我會彈了,但彈得不熟。"過了幾天,孔子已經彈得流暢動聽了,但他還不滿意,對老師說:"這支曲子的神韻我還沒領會,讓我再練習幾天吧。"又過了幾天,老師說:"現在你彈得完美無缺,可見你已經領會曲子的韻味了。咱們練習新曲子吧。"可孔子卻說:"我還沒有體會出作曲者是誰,他是個什麼樣的人呢!"接著又埋頭彈起來。直到有一天,孔子跑到老師面

[①] "六經"包括《詩》、《書》、《禮》、《易》、《春秋》和《樂》。

中國古代哲學

前，興奮地說："我已經能從曲子中感受到作曲者的形象了：他臉黑黑的，個子高高的，眼睛炯炯有神地望著遠方，四面八方的國家都臣服於他。除了周文王，這個人還會是誰呢？"老師聽了十分佩服，站起來行禮說："哎呀，你真了不起！我的老師教我這支曲子時，就說曲名叫《文王操》。"

孔子是多麼富有鑽研精神啊！

問題

孔子跟老師學琴時，為什麼要反復練習一支曲子而不學習新曲子呢？

生詞

zhòng ní 仲尼	Zhongni (another name of Confucius)	shén yùn 神韻	romantic charm
zhǔ zhāng 主張	view; proposition	wán měi wú quē 完美無缺	perfect
biān dìng 編訂	compile	lǐng huì 領會	comprehend; understand
jīng yì qiú jīng 精益求精	constantly perfect one's skill	jiǒng jiǒng yǒu shén 炯炯有神	(of eyes) bright and piercing
liú chàng 流暢	smooth	zuān yán 鑽研	study intensively

 *English Translation*

Lesson One

Confucius' Ideas

Confucius (551 B.C.—479 B.C.) was a great Chinese thinker and educator. He was a Chinese saint, a contemporary of the Greek Socrates and Indian Sakyamuni. His philosophy and thoughts have deeply influenced not only China, but also the entire world. Confucious' ideas have been developed into a school of philosophy known as Confucianism.

Throughout his life, Confucius strived to educate people on how they can be good and virtuous. He told them that in order to be a person with high moral virtues, he must be able to do the following actions.

Firstly, Confucius believed that the person must "love others." When asked by a student what "benevolence (*ren*)" meant, Confucius explained that it is to "love others." "Benevolence" implies the highest virtue. In his opinion, the most basic and most noble quality of mankind is to love others. Only a person who can love others can be considered virtuous. Loving others requires sincerity; it cannot be hypocritical. To love others, we first love our parents, siblings, and our friends because these are the people who we meet daily and know us most intimately. Beginning with our love for our family members, we should spread that love to the people around us, and to all mankind and all other things, including the entire universe.

It is easy to love our family members sincerely, but to truly love everyone and everything else is a very hard thing to do. Everyone has their own likes and dislikes. To be able to love all people and all things requires attaining a high spiritual state, in which one regards the entire world as a big family. Zhang Zai, a man who lived during the Song Dynasty, once said, "Heaven is my father, Earth is my mother, all people are my brothers and sisters, and all things are my kind." Cheng Hao, who lived during the same period, said, "The entire universe is one life, in which everything is connected, like flesh and blood. Such a connection is called 'benevolence', to sever this connection is the opposite of 'benevolence.' Only a person who immerses himself in the whole universe and loves everything as much as his own life can possess the highest virtue." All of these thoughts originated from Confucius' ideas.

The second quality the person should possess according to Confucius is that of "loyalty and forbearance." "Loyalty (*zhong*)" means faithfully trying one's best to help others while "forbearance (*shu*)" refers to being lenient and tolerant of others. Confucius said, "To desire to sustain oneself, one must sustain others; to desire to develop oneself, one should develop others too." He also said, "Do not do to others what you do not wish yourself." Everyone hopes to find happiness and joy, as well as to enjoy success in their careers. No one wants to experience misfortune, suffering, and failure. Therefore, a virtuous person should help others obtain happiness, joy, and success, and avoid misfortune, suffering, and failure. If one hopes to receive, they should help others receive; one should also help others avoid situations which they want to avoid. One should treat others the way they would like others to treat them. This is, in short, "the principle of loyalty and forbearance."

Thirdly, the person should "exercise self-restraint and return to propriety." "To exercise self-restraint (*keji*)" means to restrain one's own desire and restricting one's behavior; "to return to propriety (*fuli*)" is to comply with all social standards and norms. To achieve a stable society, man has to establish standards and norms to moderate people's conduct. A moral person should observe all these social conventions, bringing benefit to the society instead of creating social disorder.

Confucius provided a wealth of thoughts in teaching people how to be the ideal man, and these three ideas above were the most important principles that he taught. If people try their best to follow them, they will surely be able to become men of virtue.

A Brief Introduction to Confucius

Confucius, whose real name was Kong Qiu, and whose nickname was Zhongni, was born in the state of Lu during the Spring and Autumn Period. He was a famous educator, thinker, and the founder of Confucianism. Once the acting minister of Lu, he later visited many other states, trying to espouse his political views but he did not see them implemented. Confucius spent his last years collecting the ancient classics, compiling and editing several valuable books such as the Six Disciplines1 . He had indeed contributed greatly to the development of Chinese culture.

Confucius' Persistence with Learning

Since young, Confucius had always been very fond of learning. Whenever he encountered difficult questions, he would ask others for help and would not stop asking unless he understood the answer clearly. Not only did he constantly try to acquire knowledge, he also aimed to perfect his skills.

Confucius once learned how to play the *guqin* (a musical instrument) from a teacher. After practicing a piece of music for about 10 days, his teacher said satisfactorily, "You've done a good job. You may start to learn a new piece." But Confucius was not satisfied, and said, "I can play this piece of music but my skills need to be improved." A few days later, the music Confucius played had become very pleasant to listen to. However, he was still not satisfied. He said to the teacher, "I'm still not able to fully grasp the charm of this piece of music. Please allow me a few more days to practice." Several days passed and the teacher suggested, "Now you play it perfectly. I see that you've comprehended its essence. Let's practice a new piece of music." Confucius answered, "I've yet to visualize who the composer is and what he is like." Then he began to play the *guqin* again. He played the same music for many days until one day, he ran to the teacher and said with great excitement, "I can imagine who the composer is now! He is tall, has a swarthy complexion, with a pair of bright and piercing eyes. He is looking into the distance and all the states around pledge allegiance to him. Who else could it be except for Wen Wang (the ruler of Zhou)?" Upon hearing this, the teacher felt so much admiration for him that he bowed to Confucius, exclaiming, "You are incredible! When I learned this music, my teacher told me that it was indeed titled 'Wen Wang Cao.'"

From this, we can definitely see Confucius' intense drive for learning.

第二課

孟子的思想

孟子（前372—前289）是中國重要的哲學家、思想家，是孔子思想的主要繼承人之一，被中國人尊稱為"亞聖"（第二聖人）。他主要繼承了孔子"仁者愛人"的思想，對人為什麼有道德，為什麼會愛人的問題做了理論上的說明。

孟子像

一、"四端"。孔子說，人應該有道德，應該愛人。人為什麼會有道德？為什麼會愛人呢？孟子回答說，因為人有"四端"。"端"是起點、開始的意思。孟子說的"四端"，是指道德的四個起點。這四個起點是"惻隱之心"、"羞惡(wù)之心"、"辭讓之心"、"是非之心"。"惻隱之心"就是同情心；"羞惡之心"就是做了錯事、壞事會感到羞恥；"辭讓之心"就是懂得謙讓；"是非之心"就是能分別對錯和善惡。孟子認為"四端"是人生來就有的，是人與其他動物的根本區別。"四端"發展起來，就會成為四種美德："惻隱之心"會發展成為愛人（仁），"羞惡之心"會發展成為正義（義①），"辭讓之心"會發展成為有禮貌（禮），"是非之心"會發展成為明善惡（智）。

這四種"心"怎樣纔能順利地發展起來呢？孟子說："心勿忘，勿助長。""勿忘"就是不要忘記它們，要像對待幼苗那樣愛護它們。"勿助長"就是不要急於求成。孟子講過一個故事：一個農民栽了一片禾苗，第二天他見禾苗沒有長高，心裏有些著急。第三天見禾苗還沒有長高，心裏更著急了，於是他就把禾苗一棵一棵地都拔高了一點。到了第四天，所有的禾苗都死了。這就是"拔苗助長"的故事。人的道德品質是逐漸(jiàn)培養起來的，既要不間斷地努力，又不要拔苗助長。

二、"仁政"。和孔子一樣，孟子也認為在各種美德中"愛人"是最重要、最根本的。只有能真心愛人的人，對別人有一顆愛心的人，纔是真正有道德的人。一個國家的領導人更需要有這樣的道德，他必須對人民有一顆愛心。國家的領導人應該"老吾老以及人之老，幼吾幼以及人之幼"。意思是說，國家領導人愛自己的父親和母親，也要愛別人的父

---

① 孟子說的"義"是指行為正當，符合(fú)道德規範，與通常說的"正義"意思不完全相同。

親和母親；愛自己的兒女，也要愛別人的兒女。自己想生活得幸福快樂，也要讓所有的人都能生活得幸福快樂。人民是國家的基礎，只有愛人民的人纔能得到人民的擁護和愛戴，只有得到了人民的擁護和愛戴纔有資格當國家的領導人。用一顆愛人之心去管理國家就叫做"仁政"。

生詞

lǐ lùn 理論	theory	duì dài 對待	treat
cè yǐn 惻隱	commiseration; compassion	zāi 栽	plant; grow
tóngqíng 同情	sympathize with	péi yǎng 培養	cultivate; foster
xiū chǐ 羞恥	shame	gēn běn 根本	essential; core
qiānràng 謙讓	modest and humble	lǐng dǎo 領導	lead
shàn è 善惡	good and evil	rén mín 人民	people
qū bié 區別	distinguish	yōng hù 擁護	advocate; support
zhèng yì 正義	righteous	ài dài 愛戴	love; hold in high esteem
shùn lì 順利	smoothly; favorably	zī gé 資格	qualification

聽寫

對待　理論　人民　順利　領導　同情　善惡　正義

栽　培養　*端　羞恥

比一比

羞 { 羞恥 / 羞惡 }　　順 { 順利 / 順序 }　　待 { 對待 / 等待 }　　資 { 資格 / 資源 }

養 { 培養 / 營養 }　　非 { 是非 / 非常 }　　德 { 道德 / 德國 }　　護 { 擁護 / 保護 }

詞語運用

同情

詩歌《賣炭翁》表達了白居易對窮人的同情。

奶奶是一個很有同情心的人，別人有困難她總是幫忙。

愛護

我們班的同學都很愛護公共財物。

老師告訴我們要愛護動物。

人類要愛護自然環境。

說明

你總把三看成五,説明你很粗心。

你遲到了,請説明原因。

對待

對待朋友要真誠,不能虛情假意。

多音字

jiàn
間

jiàn
間斷

jiān
間

jiān
一間房

根據課文回答問題

1. 孟子是什麼時期的人?

2. 為什麼稱孟子為"亞聖"?

3. 請解釋孟子思想中"四端"的意思:"惻隱之心"、"羞惡之心"、"辭讓之心"、"是非之心"。

4. 什麼是"心勿忘,勿助長"?

詞語解釋

是非——正確與錯誤，善與惡。

愛護——愛惜並保護。

間斷——中間斷開，不連接；不連續。

急於求成——想要馬上就實現或馬上就成功。

說明——解釋明白；解釋意義的話；證明。

閱讀

孟子簡介

孟子名軻(kē)，戰國時期魯國人，中國重要的哲學家、思想家，是孔子思想的主要繼承人之一。

孟母教子

孟子小的時候，並不愛學習。他成天跑到離家不遠的一個墓地去玩，學著挖坑埋葬死人，有時連飯都忘了回家吃。於是孟母決定搬家，以免兒子再到墓地去玩。孟母把家搬到街市的附近去，但是沒想到，孟子又跟著商人上街去學著叫賣。孟母發現後，覺得這個住處也不好。最後孟母把家搬到一所學堂旁邊，孟子便開始進學堂讀書了。

孟子雖然上了學堂讀書，但是並不努力，不專心，很貪玩，經常遲到早退，使母親很擔憂。一天，孟母正在家中織布，又見到孟子很早就從學堂跑回了家。孟母問道："你為什麼回來這麼早？"孟子撒謊說："不早，跟平時一樣呀！"孟母聽完兒子的回答非常痛心，便拿起剪刀，把織布機上的紗線一下子剪斷，再也不說什麼，只坐在一旁落淚。孟子見到這種情景，內心十分難過。這時，孟母語重心長地對兒子說："要你好好讀書，是希望你能成才。像你現在這樣，總是還沒到放學的時候就不學了，這不就等於剪斷紗線，讓我織不成布嗎？"孟子聽完母親的話，眼淚直流。他從此努力學習，終於成為"亞聖"。

王金泰 畫

生詞

學堂 xué táng	school	
貪玩 tān wán	be crazy about play	
早退 zǎo tuì	leave early	
撒謊 sā huǎng	tell a lie	
紗線 shā xiàn	yarn	
語重心長 yǔ zhòng xīn cháng	(to say sth.) with great concern or in all earnestness	
等於 děng yú	be equal to; be the same as	

Lesson Two

Mencius' Ideas

Mencius (372 B.C.—289 B.C.) was an important Chinese philosopher and thinker. One of the principal followers of Confucianism, he was honored as "the Junior Sage" (the Second Saint) in China. He mainly elaborated on Confucius' idea that "benevolence consists of loving others," and made a theoretical explanation why individuals should be virtuous and why people should love others.

Firstly he talked about the concept of "four beginnings (*siduan*)." Confucius said that people should be virtuous and love others, but one may wonder why they should be virtuous and why they should love others. In Mencius' opinion, all men in their original nature possess "four beginnings (*siduan*)," "*duan*" being the starting point or the beginning. What Mencius meant by the "four beginnings" are these four principles of virtue: feelings of "commiseration," "shame and dislike," "modesty and yielding," and "right and wrong." "The feeling of commiseration" means to be sympathetic, "the feeling of shame and dislike" refers to feeling ashamed after doing something that is wrong or bad, "the feeling of modesty and yielding" denotes knowing how to be polite and humble, and "the feeling of right and wrong" suggests the ability to distinguish good from evil. Mencius believed that these "four beginnings" are innate, and that this is a fundamental difference between man and other animals. According to him, if these "four beginnings" are developed, they can become four virtues where "the feeling of commiseration" enables people to love others (which can be called "*ren*"—benevolence), "the feeling of shame and dislike" can make people righteous (that is "*yi*"[1]—righteousness), "the feeling of modesty and yielding" could develop into politeness (this is called "*li*"—propriety), and "the feeling of right and wrong" could become an ability to distinguish between good and evil (that is "*zhi*"—wisdom).

However, how can these four feelings be developed smoothly? Mencius suggests that we bear this motto in mind, "Never forget; never hasten." "Never forget" means that people should keep these feelings in mind and care for them as if they were seedlings, and "never hasten" implies that people should not rush and settle for a quick success. Mencius illustrated this in a story where he spoke of a farmer who once planted some seedlings in a rice field. The next day, the farmer went to examine the seedlings and grew worried when he saw that they were not growing taller. On the third day, he still did not observe any growth in the seedlings, and became extremely anxious. He decided to take matters into his own hands and pulled up each seedling little by little. By the fourth day, all the seedlings had died. This is the story of "*ba miao zhu zhang*," which implies that one's virtues have to be cultivated gradually. Not only does this story teach that constant effort is required, it also means that some activities may rush results, causing an adverse outcome and hence, should be avoided.

---

1 "*Yi*" mentioned here by Mencius refers to proper behaviors which usually conform to moral standards, different from "being righteous" in conventional sense.

Secondly he believed in "benevolent governance (*renzheng*)." Like Confucius, Mencius also believed that "loving others" is the most important and fundamental virtue to have among all the other virtues. Only those who can love others sincerely and have a heart for others are truly virtuous people. A nation's leader is one who especially needs to have this virtue as he has to have a loving heart for his people. He should "treat the aged in his family as they should be treated, and extend this treatment to the elderly in other people's families; treat the young in his family as they should be treated, and extend this treatment to the young of other people's families as well." This principle means that the leader should love his people's parents, sons, and daughters as much as his own parents, sons, and daughters. Only those who can make others happy will be able to live a truly happy life. Since people are the foundation of a nation, only those who love their people will receive the people's support and love, and only those who receive the people's support and love are qualified to lead the nation. Therefore, to govern a nation with a loving heart is to use this principle of "benevolent governance."

A Brief Introduction to Mencius

Mencius, whose original name was Meng Ke, was born in the state of Lu during the Warring States Period. He was an important Chinese philosopher and thinker, and one of the main followers of Confucius' ideas.

Mencius' Mother Educates Her Son

When Mencius was a little boy, he did not like to study at all. He always went to play at a cemetery near his home and learned how to dig holes to bury the dead, sometimes even forgetting to go back home for meals. Therefore, Mencius' mother decided to move to prevent her son from playing at the cemetery any further. She moved their house from beside the cemetery to beside a marketplace. Unexpectedly, Mencius, however, followed some merchants to the marketplace and learned how to hawk wares. When Mencius' mother found out about this, she felt that the marketplace was not an ideal location to educate her child. Finally, she moved to a place beside a school, where Mencius started going to school to study.

Although Mencius went to school, he still did not concentrate on his studies. Instead, he wanted to play all day long, and frequently went to school late and left school early. This worried his mother very much. One day, when Mencius' mother was weaving cloth at home, Mencius came back from school earlier than usual. She asked him, "Why did you come back so early?" Mencius lied, "It's not early, it's the same as usual." Upon hearing these words, Mencius' mother felt so heartbroken that she took up a pair of scissors and cut off the yarn on the weaving machine in her anger. She then sat there and wept silently. When Mencius saw this, he was very upset. After a while, his mother said to him with great concern, "My son, I wish that you would study hard because I hope that you can become a useful person. But if you behave like this, always leaving before school is over, isn't it the same as cutting the yarn and never being able to finish weaving the cloth?" Mencius heard his mother's words and tears ran down his cheeks. Thereafter, he studied very hard and eventually became known as "the Junior Sage."

第三課

荀子的思想

荀子（約前313—前238）是中國重要的思想家、哲學家，孔子思想的主要繼承人之一。他和孟子雖然都是孔子思想的繼承者，但他的思想卻與孟子的思想有很大的區別。

一、性惡論。孔子沒有明確說過人性是善還是惡，他認為人的本性並沒有太大的差別，不同的習慣纔使人與人之間出現了差別。孟子認為人生來就有"四端"，"四端"發展起來就成了四種美德，這叫做"性善論"。荀子認為孟子的說法是不對的，他說："人之性，惡；其善者，偽也。""偽"就是人為的努力。為什麼這樣說呢？因為人生來就有各種慾望，就有為自己求利益的本能，這些本能就是人性。如果順著這些本能發展下去，人與人之間就會發生爭鬥，所以說人性是惡的。不過人能學習，能接受教育，通過學習和接受教育就會具有道德。因此，治理國家不能只靠一

荀子像

顆愛心，而要制定完善的制度和法規。

二、"明於天人之分"。"天"就是自然界。"明於天人之分"就是分清什麼是自然界的性質和功能，什麼是人的性質和功能。荀子認為，自然界是運動變化的、有規律的，它的運動變化並沒有什麼目的，也不會按照人的願望去改變。它的功能就是使萬物自然地生長。自然界中的各種事物都相互聯繫、相互依靠，每一種事物都以其他事物為營養，它自己又是其他事物的營養。

人雖然也是自然界中的一種物，但人要比其他的自然物更有力量。人不是生來就有道德的，但人生來就有理性。人的理性分為兩個方面：一個方面是人能認識自然、利用自然、改造自然。人不長毛，不能禦寒，但人會織布，會做衣服；人沒有鋒利的爪牙，但人能製造和使用武器；人的力量小，走路慢，但人能製造車船。另一方面是人能組織成群體，組織成社會，能利用集體的力量戰勝其他事物。有了這兩點，人就成了世界上最偉大的事物了。

人雖然能認識自然、利用自然、改造自然，但是人的力量並不是無限的。人應該認識到什麼是人力能做到的，什麼是受自然規律控制的、人力改變不了的。人應該努力發揮自己的能力去認識世界和改造世界，但是不要企圖認識自己不

能認識的東西，不要企圖改變自己不能改變的東西，這就叫做"明於天人之分"。

生詞

荀子 xún zǐ	Xun Zi (name)	依靠 yī kào	rely on
偽 wěi	false; fake	改造 gǎi zào	change; transform
具有 jù yǒu	have; possess	禦寒 yù hán	keep out the cold
制度 zhì dù	system	鋒利 fēng lì	sharp
性質 xìng zhì	nature	組織 zǔ zhī	organize
功能 gōngnéng	function	社會 shè huì	society
規律 guī lǜ	law; regular pattern	集體 jí tǐ	collective
目的 mù dì	aim; purpose	發揮 fā huī	exert
聯繫 lián xì	connection	企圖 qǐ tú	attempt

聽寫

聯繫　依靠　改造　社會　組織　制度　目的　規律

具有　*企圖　發揮

比一比

規 { 法規 / 規律 }　　能 { 能力 / 功能 }　　{ 制（制度）/ 製（製造）}

具 { 具有 / 工具 }　　質 { 性質 / 品質 }　　改 { 改造 / 改變 }

組 { 組織 / 小組 }　　企 { 企圖 / 企鵝 }　　揮 { 發揮 / 揮手 }

詞語運用

規律　　法規

水在零度結冰是自然規律。

他每天早上七點起床，晚上十點睡覺，生活很有規律。

學開車一定要先學交通法規。

制度　　製造

要遵守學校的制度，上課不遲到。

這輛車是中國製造的。

聯繫

請你一定回個信,不然咱們就會失去聯繫。

這是我的電話號碼(mǎ),有事請與我聯繫。

目的

你知道他這樣做有什麼目的嗎?

近義詞

區別——辨別　　　企圖——打算

反義詞

真——偽　　　集體——個人

多音字

的 de　　　的 dì
我的 de　　　目的 dì

根據課文回答問題

1. 荀子是什麽時期的哲學家？

2. 荀子"性惡論"的内容是什麽？

3. 孟子"性善論"的内容是什麽？

4. 請解釋荀子"明於天人之分"的觀點。

相配詞語連線

戰勝　　　　教育

接受　　　　高尚

制定　　　　秩序

品德　　　　敵人

破壞　　　　法規

閱讀

荀子簡介

荀子名況，戰國末期趙國人，中國古代重要的思想家之一。荀子認為人性本惡，必須用禮儀、刑罰來約束人的行為。他還認為自然界有它自己的運行規律。他著有《荀子》一書。

《荀子‧勸學》選讀

（一）鍥而不捨

良馬跳躍一下，達不到十步遠；劣馬拉十天車卻能走很遠的路程，這是不停地走的結果。雕刻一樣東西，用刀子刻幾下就停止，朽木也刻不斷；不停地刻下去，纔能將金石雕刻成器。這說明只有堅持下去，有恒心，纔能把事情做成功。

（二）不積跬步，無以至千里；不積細流，無以成江海

如果走路不一步一步地積累，就不能達到千里之遠；不匯集細小的水流，就不能成為江海。這說明學習必須一點一點地積累，也說明事情的成功都是由小到大逐漸積累的。

生詞

xíng fá 刑罰	punishment; penalty	xiǔ mù 朽木	rotten wood
qiè ér bù shě 鍥而不捨	work with persistence	jiān chí 堅持	insist on; persist
tiào yuè 跳躍	jump; leap; bound	kuǐ bù 跬步	half a step; small or short step
diāo kè 雕刻	carve	jī lěi 積累	accumulate

Lesson Three

Xun Zi's Ideas

Xun Zi (about 313 B.C.—238 B.C.) was an important thinker and philosopher in China and also one of the main followers of Confucius' theories, but his ideas are quite different from that of Mencius'. They are as discussed below.

Firstly he talked about "the evilness of human nature." Confucius was not clear on the matter of whether human nature is good or evil. He believed that people are similar by nature and that different habits distinguish one person from another. Mencius however believed that man is born with "four beginnings," which can be developed into four virtues. This is also known as "the goodness of human nature." However, Xun Zi disagreed with Mencius. He said, "The nature of man is evil and his goodness is only acquired through training." Here, "*wei*" means acquired. Why did Xun Zi say that? In his opinion, man is born with various inherent desires and a particular relish to do things only for his own profit. These instincts are part of human nature and if men are led by those instincts, struggles would inevitably arise. Hence, he concluded that human nature is evil. However, he also believed that man can learn and receive education, and gradually become a person with moral principles. Thus, governing a nation does not rely merely on having a heart of love, a complete and sound system and legislation must be established.

Secondly he made "a distinction between heaven and man." Here, "*tian* (heaven)" refers to Nature. This theory suggests that the nature and function of Nature and man should be distinguished. Xun Zi believed that Nature is ever moving and changing, and has its own regular pattern that is without any particular purpose, being independent of man's will. Its function is to help all things grow naturally. Everything in Nature is interconnected and mutually dependent; that as it feeds on others, they are also fed on by others.

Man is one part of Nature but he is more powerful than all other things in Nature. He is not born virtuous but he is born with rationality, which has two aspects. One aspect is his ability to know Nature, use Nature, and to transform Nature. Although he cannot grow fur, man can weave cloth to make clothes to protect himself against the cold; although he does not have sharp claws, man can make and use weapons for protection; although he is weak and walks slowly, man can build ships and vehicles for travel. Another aspect is man's ability to organize people into groups and form a society, and which by doing so he gathers collective strength to overcome difficulties. Thus, with these two aspects, man is now the greatest entity in the world.

However, man's power is not limitless although he knows Nature, uses Nature, and transforms Nature. Man must know what he can accomplish with human effort and what is governed by natural laws which cannot be changed by human effort. Man must exert his own effort and try to know and transform Nature, but not attempt to know what he cannot know or change something that is beyond his ability. This is the essence of "a distinction being made between heaven and man."

A Brief Introduction to Xun Zi

Xun Zi, whose original name is Xun Kuang, was born in the state of Zhao at the end of the Warring States Period. He was one of the most important thinkers in ancient China. Xun Zi believed that human nature is evil and that man's behavior needed to be restricted by etiquette and punishment. In addition, he held the belief that Nature has its own laws of movement. All of these ideas are recorded in his monograph titled *Xun Zi*.

Excerpts from *On Study in Xun Zi*

1. To Be Persistent

Even a strong horse cannot leap further than 10 strides, but a weak horse can cover a long distance if it keeps on dragging the cart for 10 days. It is the continuous effort put in that makes the difference. When we want to carve something, but if we stop only after a few tries, not even rotten wood would be cut. However, with continuous effort and persistence, metal and stone can not only be cut, but carved into different shapes and sizes. This illustrates the truth that success will come only if you persist and work with perseverance.

2. A Thousand *Li* is Covered Step by Step; Rivers and Seas are Formed by A Thousand Streams

You will not reach as far as a thousand *li*, if you do not continue walking step by step; there will be no rivers or seas, if a thousand streams do not flow and merge together. Such facts illustrates the truth that knowledge is obtained through gradual effort, and success is achieved by accumulating small gains.

第四課

墨子的思想

墨子（約前475—前396）是中國重要的思想家、哲學家。他創立了墨家學派。墨子和他的學生大多數是手工業者，他們都很重視勞動和勞動成果，經常討論勞動問題。墨子認為，人與其他的動物不同。其他的動物以身上長的毛為衣服，以蹄爪為鞋子，以自然的水草為飲料和飯菜，所以它們不用勞動就能生存。人是不同的，人必須通過勞動纔能有衣服穿、有飯菜吃，通過勞動纔能生存，因此每一個人都應該勞動。一個人到別人的果園裏去偷水果，這樣的行為對不對呢？當然是不對的，因為他沒有勞動而佔有別人的勞動成果。人只有參加勞動纔能享受勞動成果，不勞而獲是不道德的。

墨子像

一、"兼相愛"。"兼相愛"就是人與人之間互相愛。墨子也認為人的最高道德是愛人，但他說的愛人和孔子、孟子所說的愛人不一樣。孔子、孟子所說的愛人是一種有差別的愛。他們主張要先愛自己的父母，再愛別人的父母；先愛自己的親人，再愛別人的親人；愛自己的父母要比愛別人的父母多一些，愛自己的親人要比愛別人的親人多一些。這叫做"愛有差等"。墨子主張愛人不應該有差別，愛別人的國家就像愛自己的國家一樣，愛別人的父母就像愛自己的父母一樣，愛別人就像愛自己一樣。愛人應該從自己做起，自己要先去愛別人，別人纔會愛自己；自己要先去愛別人的父母，別人纔會愛自己的父母；自己要先去愛別人的國家，別人纔會愛自己的國家。如果人與人之間，家與家之間，國與國之間都能互相愛，世界上就沒有爭奪，沒有戰爭了。

　　二、"交相利"。"交相利"就是互利。墨子認為，判斷一個人的行為是不是道德的，不僅要看他的行為動機，還要看他的行為效果。只有以愛人為動機並且能給人帶來實際利益的行為纔是有道德的行為。因此他認為"兼相愛"應該體現在"交相利"上，就是體現為人與人之間的互利。墨子主張，人與人之間要互相幫助，強壯的人要幫助弱小的人，富人要幫助窮人，有知識的人要幫助沒有知識的人，要讓那些沒有妻子兒女的老人和失去了父母的孤兒有所依靠，要讓所有的人都能過上好生活。無論是國家還是個人，以大欺小，以強欺弱，以富欺貧都是不道德的。

生詞

chéng guǒ 成果	achievement	zhēng duó 爭奪	fight for
tǎo lùn 討論	discuss	hù lì 互利	of mutual benefit
yǐn liào 飲料	drinks; beverage	dòng jī 動機	motive; intention
shēng cún 生存	survive	xiào guǒ 效果	effect
zhàn yǒu 佔有	own; possess	tǐ xiàn 體現	embody; reflect
xiǎng shòu 享受	enjoy	zhǔ zhāng 主張	advocate; proposition
jiān 兼	simultaneously; concurrently		

聽寫

主張　生存　享受　飲料　體現　互利　動機　討論

效果　成果　*爭奪　兼

比一比

存 { 生存 / 存在 }　　動 { 動機 / 運動 }　　現 { 發現 / 體現 }

果 { 效果 / 成果 }　　飲 { 飲料 / 飲用 }　　{ 佔（佔有）/ 站（站立）}

詞語運用

討論
大家可以討論一下，這件事情到底應該怎麼辦。

主張
眼看要來不及了，他主張馬上就走。

我們大家都贊成你的主張。

享受

不愛勞動光愛享受可不好。

假日人們來到海邊,享受陽光、沙灘和新鮮的空氣。

效果

你的動機雖好,但是方法不當(dàng),效果大打折扣。

我吃過這種藥,效果不錯。

天天游泳,減肥效果明顯。

根據課文回答問題

1. 墨子創立了什麼學派?
2. 請解釋墨子"兼相愛"的觀點。
3. 墨子的"兼相愛"與孔子的"愛人"有什麼不同?
4. 請解釋墨子"交相利"的觀點。

詞語解釋

不勞而獲——自己不勞動而取得別人的勞動成果。

> 閱讀

墨子簡介

墨子名翟,戰國時期魯國人,墨家學派創始人,曾在宋國當過官。他主張勤勞、克苦、為他人,反對諸侯相互吞併的戰爭,提出"兼愛"、"非攻"等主張,著有《墨子》一書。

墨子救宋

公元前440年,楚國準備用魯班製造的雲梯攻打宋國。墨子聽到消息後,一面派弟子三百餘人趕往宋國,幫助宋國守城,一面親自趕往楚國去說服楚王停止這場戰爭。墨子一路辛苦,走了十天十夜,終於來到楚國。

他見了楚王,說:"現在有一個人,他自己有漂亮的車子,還去偷鄰居家破爛的車子;他自己有絲綢綉衣,還去偷鄰居家破舊的衣衫;他自己有精美的肉食,還去偷鄰居家粗糙的飯菜。這算是什麼人呢?"楚王說:"這個人一定是犯了偷竊的毛病。"墨子接著說:"我聽說您準備攻打宋國,與這個偷竊鄰居的人有什麼不同呢?如果攻打宋國,您必定失去了'義'而得不到宋。"墨子的話使楚王猶豫起來。

過了一會兒,楚王說:"魯班已為我造好了攻城的雲梯,我還是想攻打宋國。"於是墨子解下身上的皮帶當做城池,用一些小木板與魯班"演練"了一場攻守戰。魯班用雲梯攻城,墨子守

城,最後,魯班"戰敗"。魯班說:"我還有辦法,可是我不說。"墨子說:"我知道你的辦法,我也不說。"他們的對話楚王沒有聽明白,便問道:"你們這是什麼意思?"墨子說:"魯班不過是要大王殺我。他以為殺了我,宋國就無法守城了。其

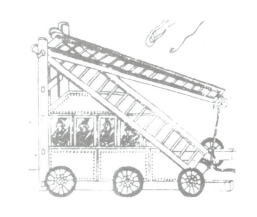

實,我的三百多名弟子已經到宋國做好守城的準備了。您就是殺了我,楚國也打不了勝仗。"楚王聽了以後,終於放弃了對宋國的戰爭。

　　墨子救宋的故事,是墨家學派"兼愛"、"非攻",主張和平的體現。

生詞

mò dí 墨翟	Mo Di (name)		pí dài 皮帶	leather belt
zhū hóu 諸侯	duke or prince		yǎn liàn 演練	drill; practise
tōu qiè 偷竊	steal		fàng qì 放弃	give up; quit
yóu yù 猶豫	hesitate		zhì zhǐ 制止	stop

Lesson Four

Mo Zi's Ideas

Mo Zi (about 475 B.C.—396 B.C.) was an important Chinese thinker and philosopher. He founded a new philosophy called Mohism. Mo Zi, along with the majority of his students, were handicraftsmen and often discussed the issue of labor. They placed great emphasis on labor and the result of labor. In Mo Zi's opinion, man is different from other animals. Other animals have fur and feathers as clothes, claws, and paws as shoes, grass and water as food and drinks, and can thus survive without labor. But man is different. Only by working can he be clothed and fed, and it is only through labor that he can survive. Therefore, it is a must that everyone works. Is it right for a person to steal fruits from another's orchard? Of course it is wrong, because in doing so, he has tried to possess the fruit of other people's labor without doing any work himself. Man can only enjoy the result of labor by doing the work himself. It is immoral to gain without pain. Mo Zi's main thoughts are discussed below.

Firstly, Mo Zi believed in "universal love." This means that people should love each other. Like Confucius and Mencius, Mo Zi believed that the greatest virtue one can have is to love others, but his idea differed from the "partiality of love" put forth by Confucius and Mencius. Confucius and Mencius held the belief that people love their own parents first, then the parents of others; that they love their own immediate family members before loving others' family members. They believed that people love their parents and their family members more than others' parents and relatives. This is known as the "partiality of love." But Mo Zi argued that there should be no partiality in loving people. People should love other nations as much as their own nation; they should love others' parents as much as their own parents; they should love others as themselves. Mo Zi believed that love has to start with oneself. People should love others first before they can receive love from others; people should love the parents of others, then others will love their parents; people should love the nations of others first before others can love their nations. If there is love between people, families, and nations, there would be no fights and wars in the world.

The second principle Mo Zi espoused was that of "mutual benefit." "Mutual benefit" means to derive benefit from each other. Mo Zi claimed that in order to judge whether a person's behavior is moral or not, one must observe not only the motivation of his actions, but also the results of his actions. An action is considered moral only when it is motivated by one's love for others and if it brings people actual benefits at the same time. Thus, "universal love" should be embodied in "mutual benefit," that is, universal love is reflected in the mutual benefits people derive from each other. Mo Zi advocated that people should help each other: the strong should help the weak, the rich should help the poor, and the learned should help the illiterate, so that the old who are without family and the orphans who have lost their parents can have a source of support, and everyone will be able to live a good life. Whether as a nation or a person, it is immoral for the big, the strong, and the rich to bully the small, the weak, and the poor.

A Brief Introduction to Mo Zi

Mo Zi, whose given name is Di, was born in the state of Lu during the Warring States Period. He was the founder of Mohism and was an official in the state of Song. He advocated diligence, hard work, and altruism, and condemned offensive wars between different states. He proclaimed ideas of "universal love," "condemnation of war," etc. All of these ideas are recorded in his monograph titled *Mo Zi*.

Mo Zi Saves the State of Song

In 440 B.C., the state of Chu decided to attack the state of Song using Lu Ban's cloud ladders. Upon hearing the news, Mo Zi immediately sent about 300 disciples to Song to help protect the city while he hurried to Chu to try to persuade the King of Chu to stop the war. It was a very tiring trip; he walked for 10 days and 10 nights before finally arriving at Chu.

Mo Zi met the King of Chu and said, "Now, there is a person who has a beautiful carriage but he steals his neighbor's damaged cart; he has splendid silk clothes, but he steals his neighbor's shabby clothes; he has very good food, but he steals his neighbor's crude food. What kind of person do you think he is?" The King of Chu answered, "He must have gotten into the habit of stealing." Mo Zi continued, "I heard that you are going to attack the state of Song. Is that any different from this person? If you attack Song, you will surely lose the virtue of 'righteousness' and not gain Song in the end." Mo Zi's words made the King of Chu hesitate.

After a while, the King of Chu said, "Lu Ban has already created the cloud ladders for me and I still want to use them to attack Song." Hence, Mo Zi removed his leather belt and used it to represent a city. Using some small boards, he engaged in simulated war games with Lu Ban. Lu Ban attacked the city using the cloud ladders while Mo Zi tried his best to defend the city. Eventually, Lu Ban was "defeated." Then Lu Ban said, "I have another method but I will not tell you what it is." Mo Zi replied, "I know your method and I won't tell either." Confused by their dialog, the King of Chu could not help asking, "What do you mean?" Mo Zi explained, "Lu Ban wants Your Majesty to kill me. He thinks that by doing so, the state of Song will no longer be able to defend itself. In fact, more than 300 of my disciples have already arrived at Song and have made preparations to defend the city. Even if you kill me, Chu cannot possibly win the war." After hearing this, the King of Chu had no other choice but to finally call off the war.

The story of how Mo Zi saved the state of Song is a representation of Mohism's "universal love," "condemnation of war," and the advocate of peaceful settlement of disputes.

第五課

老子的思想

老子（約前606—前586）是中國最重要的思想家、哲學家之一，他的思想充分體現了中國人的智慧，對東方國家甚至全世界都有很大的影響。他創立了道家學派。

一、"反者道之動"。老子的思想是圍繞著他對"道"的理解展開的。"道"就是道路，就是天地萬物都要走過的道路。用哲學語言講，"道"就是規律、法則。它的主要內容是"反者道之動"，意思是說，任

老子騎牛圖 （明）張 路

何事物都會走向自己的反面。老子認為，世界上的事物都有自己的對立面，都有一種東西和自己相反，比如大與小、多與少、高與低、前與後、長與短、生與死、成功與失敗等等。每一種事物都以自己的對立面為前提，比如沒有高就沒有低，沒有惡就沒有善，沒有假就沒有真，沒有醜就沒有

美。每一種事物發展到了頂點就會走向自己的反面，比如太陽昇到了最高點就會慢慢落下去，天氣到了最冷的時候就會逐漸變暖，人生長到了頂點就會一天天走向死亡。這條道路是每一個人、每一個事物都要走的，這是天地萬物發展變化的規律。

二、"柔弱勝剛強"。因為事物都會走向自己的反面，所以老子認為弱小的事物最有生命力，要比強大的事物更有力量，弱小的事物能夠戰勝強大的事物。他舉例說："世界上的事物沒有比水更柔弱的了，可是它最能攻破堅硬的東西。"大家都知道，水雖然很柔軟，但沒有任何東西能打破它，用刀子砍不斷它，用鐵錘砸不爛它。可是水卻能沖壞堅硬的東西。屋檐上的雨水往下滴，時間長了能把下面的石頭打出一個洞來。這就叫做"柔弱勝剛強"。無論是一個人還是一個國家，要想長期生存下去，就要保持柔弱的狀態。老子說："人活著的時候總是柔軟的，死後就變得堅硬了。花草樹木活著的時候總是柔軟的，死後就變得又乾又硬了。"同樣的道理，我們要想打敗自己的敵人，就要先讓它強大起來；我們要想奪取敵人的東西，就要先給它一些東西。任何東西都不會長久不變的，一旦它強大了，也就會逐漸衰落了。

三、"無為而無不為"。"道"不是任何一種具體的事物，可是一切事物都是從"道"中走出來的，一切事物都要按照"道"的規定生存和發展。作為一個國家的領導人，也要像"道"一樣"無為"。"無為"就是不做任何具體的事情，不管任何一個具體的部門。如果你去管理外交部，就無法管理內務部；如果你帶領軍隊去打仗，就無法去組織社會生產。一個國家的最高領導人只有不去做任何具體的事情，不去管理任何具體的部門，纔能做好所有的事情，管理好所有的部門。這就叫做"無為而無不為"。

生詞

chōng fèn 充分	full; abundant		wū yán 屋檐	eaves
wéi rào 圍繞	revolve around; center on		gáng qiáng 剛強	firm; hard
lǐ jiě 理解	understand; comprehend		bǎo chí 保持	keep; maintain
fǎ zé 法則	rule; law		duó qǔ 奪取	capture; seize
duì lì miàn 對立面	opposite; antithesis		yí dàn 一旦	once; in case
qián tí 前提	premise		jù tǐ 具體	specific; concrete
chǒu 醜	ugliness		wài jiāo 外交	diplomacy; foreign affairs
jiān yìng 堅硬	hard		nèi wù 內務	domestic affairs
róu ruǎn 柔軟	soft			

聽寫

充分　外交　具體　無論　剛強　理解　堅硬　醜　法則　*圍繞　柔弱

比一比

具 { 具體 / 具有 / 工具

持 { 保持 / 持久 / 主持

則 { 法則 / 原則

發 { 發明 / 發現

柔 { 柔軟 / 柔弱

強 { 剛強 / 強壯

提 { 前提 / 提高

頂 { 頂點 / 頂天立地

詞語運用

充分

老子的思想充分體現了中國人的智慧。

離考試還有三個星期，我有充分的時間復習功課。

一旦

一旦學生迷上電子遊戲，他的學習就會常常受到影響。

一旦下雪，上山的路就不通了。

一旦學會開車，我就自由了。

保持

同學們要注意保持教室的清潔衛生。

老師說："上課要保持安靜。"

中國乒乓球隊男子單打，連續六年保持世界冠軍。

近義詞

規律——法則　　　　無論——不論

反義詞

柔弱——剛強　　　　正面——反面

柔軟——堅硬　　　　美——醜

根據課文回答問題

1. 老子是什麼時期的人，他創立了什麼學派？

2. 老子認為："世界上的事物都有自己的對立面，都有一種東西和自己相反。"你的看法呢？

3. 請解釋下列老子的觀點："反者道之動"、"柔弱勝剛強"、"無為而無不為"。

閱讀

老子簡介

老子，春秋時期大哲學家，道家學派的創始人。他出生在楚國，姓李，名耳，字伯陽，又稱老聃。老子從小愛讀書，廣泛閱讀了各種書籍。他二十多歲時，在東周都城洛陽當上了管理國家圖書的官，後來逐漸成為知名的大學問家，著有《道德經》一書。當時常有人向他請教問題，相傳孔子曾向他問禮。

孔子問"禮"

孔子曾經專門到洛陽向老子請教"禮"的知識。孔子引用了許多古代聖賢關於禮制的話向老子請教。老子淡淡一笑，對孔子說："孔丘啊，你提到的這些古代聖賢都已經死去很久了，恐怕埋在地下的骨頭都腐爛了吧，就剩下這些話還流傳於世。所以你不必去模仿他們，用這些話約束自己的言行。君子應該有適應社會的能力，碰到機會就轟轟烈烈地幹一番事業；沒有機會就遠離政治，無拘無束地生活。你覺得是不是這個道理？"孔子聽了很受啟發。

關於老子的《道德經》

老子一直住在洛陽，周景王死後，爆發了長達五年的內戰。敗兵逃走時，帶走了圖書館許多珍貴的書籍，這讓老子很難過。他左思右想，決定去戰亂極少的秦國安度晚年。

老子騎著青牛上路了。沒走幾日，便來到了函谷關口，過了函谷關就進入秦國了。正在這時，守關的官員尹喜迎出來恭恭敬敬地向老子行禮說："先生經過這裏，沒能遠迎，希望您別見怪。先生學問廣博，見識深遠，既然路過這裏，請您小住幾日，將您的見解寫成一部書，一可讓我拜讀，二可讓天下百姓受到您的教誨，請您不要推辭！"

老子被尹喜的真摯所感動，便住下來，把自己關於道、德、無為而治、以弱勝強以及對宇宙、人生、社會等方面的見解，全部融於一書之中，寫成一部五千餘字的《道德經》。這部書最核心的內容是"道"，老子認為"道"是宇宙的本源，世界上萬事萬物的形成和發展，都由"道"轉化和生成，它像天地一樣永不停息地運動，它的規律就是自然的規律、社會的規律。

成書以後，老子繼續西行，此後他的下落就沒有人知道了。

生詞

lǎo dān 老聃	Lao Dan (a form of address for Lao Zi)	yǐn 尹	Yin (surname)
mó fǎng 模仿	emulate; imitate	jiàn guài 見怪	mind; take offense
jūn zǐ 君子	a man of noble character	guǎng bó 廣博	extensive; wide
hōng hōng liè liè 轟轟烈烈	vigorous	jiàn jiě 見解	view; opinion
wú jū wú shù 無拘無束	unrestrained	jiào huì 教誨	instructions; teachings
qǐ fā 啟發	enlighten	zhēn zhì 真摯	sincere
ān dù wǎnnián 安度晚年	enjoy the later years of life	róng...zhī zhōng 融於……之中	merge into
hán gǔ guān 函谷關	Han Gu Pass	hé xīn 核心	core; kernel
		xià luò 下落	whereabouts

 English Translation

Lesson Five

Thought of Lao Zi

Lao Zi (about 606 B.C.—586 B.C.) was one of the most important Chinese thinkers and philosophers. His thoughts fully represent the wisdom of Chinese people and has great influence on other oriental countries, and even the entire world. The philosophy he espoused came to be known as Taoism or *Tao Jia*. His main thoughts are discussed below.

Firstly, Lao Zi believed that "the movement of *Tao* is in a cycle." Lao Zi's thought revolves around his comprehension of "*Tao*." "*Tao*" means "path" or "way." It is the way in which everything must pass. In philosophical terms, "*Tao*" refers to laws and rules. Its main content is that "the movement of Tao is in a cycle," which means that everything is destined to move towards its opposite. Lao Zi held the belief that everything in the world has its own opposites, such as big and small, many and few, high and low, front and back, long and short, life and death, and success and failure. Everything exists with its opposite as its premise. For instance, if there was no "high," there would be no "low," there would be no good without evil, no truth without falsehood, and no beauty without ugliness. Everything, when it reaches its peak, will move towards its opposite, like the sun setting after rising to its highest, like the weather becoming warmer when it has reached its coldest, and like men moving towards death after living for a long time. This is the way that everybody and everything passes and the law by which everything in the world develops.

Lao Zi also subscribed to his second concept of which he says that "the soft will conquer the hard, and the weak will conquer the strong." Since things will inevitably move towards their opposites, Lao Zi believed that weak and soft things are more powerful than strong and hard things, and that the former can defeat the latter. He cited water as an example and said, "Nothing in the world is more supple than water, yet there is nothing more powerful than water in attacking that which is hard and strong." As we all know, water is very soft, but nothing can break it. It cannot be broken by either knife or hammer. Conversely, however, water can damage something that is hard and strong. If water continues to drip from eaves down onto a stone underneath for a period of time, a hole will eventually form on the stone's surface. This is, indeed, an example of "the weak overcoming and conquering the strong." Be it a person or a nation, if it hopes to survive for a long time, it must maintain its state of softness and weakness. Lao Zi said, "When alive, a man's body is supple; when dead, it becomes hard. When alive, plants are supple; when dead, they become dry and stiff." The same truth, he asserts, applies to fighting the enemy. If we want to defeat the enemy, we must let them become stronger first, and should we want to capture something from the enemy, we must give them some benefits first. There is nothing that will remain unchanged; the enemy will decline gradually once it has become extremely strong.

Lao Zi's third principle is that "by reaching the state of inaction, one can succeed in everything." "*Tao*" is not something concrete, yet everything originates from it, lives and grows by it. Therefore, a nation's leader should be inactive like the way *Tao* is. "Inaction" means doing nothing specific, managing no specific branch. If one is in charge of the Ministry of Foreign Affairs, one cannot manage the Department of Domestic Affairs; if one is leading troops to fight in battle, then one cannot organize social production. Thus, the supreme leader of a nation can manage everything and all branches well only if he does not do anything specific or manage any specific branch. This is what it means when we say "by reaching the state of inaction, one can succeed in everything."

A Brief Introduction to Lao Zi

Lao Zi was a great philosopher during the Spring and Autumn Period as well as the founder of Taoism. He was born in the state of Chu. His family name is Li, given name Er, nickname Boyang, and he is also known as "Lao Dan." Lao Zi loved reading since childhood and he read widely. In his twenties, he worked as an officer in the Imperial Library in Luoyang, the capital of the Eastern Zhou Dynasty. Later on, he gradually became a man known for his great learning and wrote a book titled

Tao Teh Ching. He was so learned that many people came to consult him about their questions. Legend claims that Confucius once discussed rites and propriety with him.

Confucius' Inquiry about "Rites"

It was said that Confucius once made a special trip to Luoyang and inquired of Lao Zi about "rites." He quoted many remarks made by great ancient men. Smiling faintly, Lao Zi told Confucius, "Kong Qiu, those great ancient men you mentioned have been dead for a long time and their bones have perhaps already decayed. Only their words have been handed down to this very day. In my opinion, it is not necessary for you to emulate them and use their words to restrict your behavior. A man of noble character should have the ability to adapt himself to society. If he chances upon an opportunity, he may achieve great success in his career; if no opportunity comes by, he may live a carefree life without politics. Do you think my words make sense?" Confucius was greatly enlightened by his words.

About Lao Zi's *Tao Teh Ching*

Lao Zi lived in Luoyang until the death of King Jing of the Zhou Dynasty when there was an outbreak of civil war that lasted five years. The defeated army took away a lot of valuable books from the Imperial Library in their retreat. This made Lao Zi very sad. After much deliberation, he decided to enjoy the later years of his life in the state of Qin, where there were fewer wars.

Riding a water buffalo, Lao Zi started on his journey. Several days later, he came to Han Gu Pass. Crossing the Pass would have brought him into the state of Qin. Just then, Yin Xi, the officer who was guarding the gate, came out and saluted Lao Zi respectfully. He said, "I'm sorry that I didn't come out to welcome you earlier. I hope you don't take offense. You are known for your extensive knowledge and farsightedness. Since you are here, I would like to invite you to stay for a few days to write a book of your opinions. Not only can I read it, the common people can also benefit from your teachings. Please do not turn me down."

Moved by Yin Xi's sincerity, Lao Zi stayed and compiled all his ideas about *Tao*, virtues, his non-action policy and theory about the weak conquering the strong, and other viewpoints about the universe, life, and society into one book entitled *Tao Teh Ching*. Comprising a total of about 5,000 Chinese characters, the core of this book is "*Tao*", which is, in Lao Zi's opinion, the origin of the universe. He believed that the growth and development of everything in the world is generated and transformed by "*Tao*," which moves constantly like heaven and earth. Its law is the law of nature, the law of society.

After Lao Zi finished writing the book, he continued his journey westward, and nobody knew of his whereabouts from then on.

第六課

莊子的思想

莊子（約前369—前286）是中國重要的思想家、哲學家，道家學派的主要代表人物之一。他的思想在中國思想史、哲學史、文學史上有很高的地位。

一、"道"。莊子的思想也是圍繞著"道"展開的，不過他對"道"的理解與老子有所不同。老子所說的"道"主要是指"反者道之動"，而莊子說的"道"主要有兩個方面：一個方面是指整個宇宙，一切事物都包括在其中；另一個方面是指宇宙的運動變化，天地萬物不停的運動變化就是"道"。莊子的"道"有兩個特徵：其一，"道"是天地萬物的全體而不是任何一種具體的事物，任何一種具體的事物都是有限的，而"道"是無限的，所以"道"是"無"而不是"有"；其二，"道"是自然而然地存在，自然而然地運動變化，一切

莊子像

事物自己的存在和變化都是"道"。

二、自然。莊子說的自然不是自然界，而是自然而然。比如颱風下雨是自然，人餓了吃飯、渴了喝水也是自然，一切非人為的存在和變化都是自然。莊子認為，世界上一切事物都是自然而然地存在著，自然而然地變化著。任何事物都有自己的本性，都有自己的生存方式，都有自己的功用。比如馬這種動物，蹄子可以踏霜雪，皮毛可以禦風寒，吃草喝水，相互戲耍，這是馬的自然，它們喜歡這樣生活。人們給馬帶上了馬鞍，讓它拉車，騎上它賽跑，訓練它，用皮鞭打它，這就破壞了馬的自然。世界上的事物都是這樣，鶴的腿很長，如果把它的腿截短了，它就不能生活了。雞的腿很短，如果把它的腿加長了，它就會因為無法吃到地上的食物而餓死。因此人應該尊重自然、順應自然，而不要按照自己的願望去改變自然、破壞自然、打擾自然。只有這樣，世界纔能更好地存在，人類纔能更好地生存。

三、自由。莊子喜歡講故事，他說："北海裏有一條大魚，魚的身體有幾千里長。大魚變成了一隻鳥，鳥的脊背有幾千里寬。大鳥要飛到南海去。它一起飛，海水被擊起了三千里高的大浪。它乘著水和空氣的力量飛到九萬里的高空，翅膀像烏雲那樣遮住天日，一直飛了六個月纔飛到南海。大鳥的飛行多麼壯觀、多麼自由啊！"可是，莊子認為這還不是真正的自由，它還需要憑借空氣和水的力量，真正的自由是無條件的。什麼樣的自由是無條件的呢？莊子說"乘天地之正，而御六氣之變，以遊無窮者"是不需要條件的。也就是說，隨著自然的變化而變化，隨著自然的運動而運動纔是無條件的自由，纔是真正的自由。這樣的人需要忘掉自己的存在，把自己融入到自然的變化中去。

王金泰 畫

生詞

dài biǎo 代表	represent	xùn liàn 訓練	train; drill
dì wèi 地位	position; status	jié duǎn 截短	cut short
zhěng gè 整個	whole; entire	shùnyìng 順應	comply with; conform to
yí qiè 一切	all; everything	dǎ rǎo 打擾	disturb; trouble
tè zhēng 特徵	features; characteristic	jǐ bèi 脊背	back
cún zài 存在	existence	píng jiè 憑借	rely on; depend on
gōngyòng 功用	function; use	tiáo jiàn 條件	condition
shuāng 霜	frost	róng rù 融入	merge
xì shuǎ 戲耍	play with		

聽寫

代表　整個　訓練　一切　地位　打擾　條件　戲耍

脊背　特徵　*霜　融入

比一比

表 { 代表 / 表演 }　　功 { 功能 / 功夫 }　　整 { 整個 / 整齊 }

順 { 順應 / 順利 }　　特 { 特徵 / 特別 }　　位 { 地位 / 位置 }

詞語運用

一切

我們已經做好了一切準備，就等著出發了。

你放心走吧，這裏一切都有人照管。

我在學校一切都好，請媽媽放心。

條件

想跟我去游泳有一個條件，要做完作業。

這裏的居住條件很好，又安全，又方便。

代表

吳霜代表我們班參加演講比賽。

近義詞

整個——全部　　　一切——所有　　　憑借——依靠

反義詞

有限——無限

根據課文回答問題

1. 莊子是什麼時期的人？是什麼學派的代表人物？

2. 什麼是莊子講的"道"？他對"道"的理解與老子有什麼不同？

3. 莊子認為："人應該尊重自然、順應自然，而不應該按照自己的願望去改變自然、破壞自然、打擾自然。這樣，世界纔能更好地存在，人類纔能更好地存在。"你的看法如何？

莊子簡介

莊子名周，宋國（今河南商丘）人，戰國時期的哲學家、文學家，道家學派的代表人物之一。莊子的文章華麗而浪漫，善於運用打比方和講故事的方法闡述道理，表達觀點。

莊子與楚王

楚威王聽說莊子很有才能，派人帶著禮物去請他到楚國當宰相。使者見到莊子，恭恭敬敬地說："我們大王聽說先生賢明能

王金泰 畫

幹，派我來請先生當楚國的宰相。"莊子微微一笑，說："宰相是個不小的官位，大王給的金錢也不少。你有沒有見過太廟裏當祭品的牛？每天餵它們大豆、青草，養得它們又肥又壯，小豬羨慕它們有這麼好的運氣。但是後來，這些牛都會被披上彩色的綢子，拉到太廟裏當祭品宰殺了。恐怕這時候它們要羨慕小豬自由自在的生活了。我寧願像小豬那樣過貧寒的自由生活，也不願做官受約束，最後還可能像那些牛一樣逃不過被殺的命運。"使者只好回到楚國去了。

生詞

chǎn shù 闡述	expound; elaborate		pī 披	drape over; wrap around
dí què 的確	indeed; really		chóu zi 綢子	silk fabric
jì pǐn 祭品	sacrifices		nìng yuàn 寧願	would rather; better
xiàn mù 羨慕	admire; envy		táo bu guò 逃不過	unable to escape

問題

莊子為什麼不願意做楚國的宰相？

 *English Translation*

Lesson Six

Zhuang Zi's Ideas

Zhuang Zi (about 369 B.C.—286 B.C.) was an important Chinese thinker and philosopher as well as one of the main representatives of the Taoist school of thought. His ideas are highly regarded in the Chinese history of philosophical thought and literature. The essence of his teaching is discussed below.

Firstly, "*Tao*." Zhuang Zi's ideas revolve around the concept of "*Tao*" as well, but his understanding of it is different from that of Lao Zi's. Lao Zi advocated that "the movement of *Tao* is in a cycle." However, when Zhuang Zi talked about "*Tao*," he refers to two aspects: one being the entire universe in which everything is included and the other is the movement and changes of the universe. The movement and changes of everything in the world constitutes "*Tao*." In Zhuang Zi's opinion, "*Tao*" has two characteristics. The first characteristic of "*Tao*" is that it is the integral whole of everything rather than anything specific which is limited and infinite, which implies "nothingness" instead of "being." The second feature about "*Tao*" is that it exists, and moves naturally. It is the existence of everything and all their changes.

Second, "naturalness." Zhuang Zi clarified that this term does not refer to Nature, but naturalness. It is, for example, natural to have wind and rain, natural for people to eat when they are hungry, and to drink when they are thirsty. All existence and changes that are not caused by man are natural, and this is what naturalness means. Zhuang Zi believed that everything in the world exists and changes in a natural way. Everything has its own nature, its own method of survival, and its own function. Take horses for an example. Their hoofs can tread frost and snow, and their fur can protect them from the cold. They graze, drink, and play with each other as they like—this is the life that they naturally like. But should people put saddles on them, and make them drive carts, ride them in races, train them or whip them, they destroy the natural behavior of a horse. That is true with all other existences. A crane with long legs cannot live if we cut its legs shorter, and a rooster will die of hunger if we make its legs longer because it would be unable to eat food on the ground. People should therefore respect Nature and not try to change, destroy, or disturb Nature according to their own wishes. It is only by doing so that the world and human beings can exist happily together.

Third, "freedom." Zhuang Zi loved to tell stories. He illustrated the concept of "freedom" in a story, "In the North Sea, there was once a big fish with a body that was a few thousand *li* long. This big fish transformed into a bird with a back that was a few thousand li wide and it intended to fly to the South Sea. As it took flight, water splashed up into the air until it reached a height of 3,000 *li*. Using the power of the water and air, the bird flew to a height of 90,000 *li*, its wings spreading like clouds covering the sun. It kept flying for six months until it arrived at the South Sea. How splendidly and

how freely it flew!" However, Zhuang Zi believed that this was not true freedom since the bird had to rely on the power of air and water. In his opinion, true freedom is unconditional. What kind of freedom is unconditional? Zhuang Zi pointed out that someone who "chariots on the normality of the universe, rides on the transformations of the six elements, and makes an excursion into infinite" enjoys unconditional freedom. In other words, true freedom, or unconditional freedom, is the freedom which can change and move along with Nature. Such freedom can only be achieved when man forgets and disregards his own existence, and starts to flow along with changes that are natural.

A Brief Introduction to Zhuang Zi

Zhuang Zi, whose real name is Zhuang Zhou, was born in the state of Song (presently known as Shangqiu of the Henan Province). Not only was he a philosopher and a man of letters during the Warring States Period, he was also one of the main representatives of the Taoist school of thought. Zhuang Zi's essays were exceptional and romantic and he was good at expressing his ideas and elaborating on his principles using metaphors and fables.

The Story of Zhuang Zi and the King of Chu

When he heard that Zhuang Zi was a very capable man, the King of Chu (Wei Wang) sent out an ambassador bearing generous gifts to invite him to be the prime minister of Chu. When he saw Zhuang Zi, the ambassador spoke to him respectfully, saying, "Our King appreciates your wisdom and abilities highly, and so he has sent me to invite you to be the prime minister of Chu." Upon hearing this, Zhuang Zi replied with a smile, "Being a prime minister is a high official post, and the money offered by the King is substantial indeed. Have you ever seen the cows that are offered as sacrifices in the Imperial Ancestral Temple? They are fed beans and green grass every day until they grow fat and strong. The piglets envy their good fortune. But eventually, all these cows will have colorful silk fabric thrown over them and sent to the Temple to be slaughtered as sacrifices. At that time, it would probably be the cows' turn to envy the freedom of the piglets. I would rather live a poor but free life like the piglets, than be an official limited by rules, and eventually be unable to escape the fate of being killed like those cows." Unable to dissuade him, the ambassador had no choice but to return to Chu alone.

第七課

孫子的思想

孫子（孔子同時代人，生卒年月不詳）是中國古代偉大的軍事家。他寫過一部書，叫做《孫子兵法》，系統地論述了戰爭中的各種問題，在世界上有很大影響。直到現在，還有許多政治家、軍事家、實業家學習它。

孫子像

一、敵我。任何戰爭都分為敵方和我方。在戰爭開始之前，最重要的工作就是要清楚地瞭解敵我雙方的情況，包括：哪一方是正義的，哪一方是非正義的；哪一方的統帥更會打仗；哪一方的地形更有利；哪一方的戰士更有訓練；哪一方的紀律更嚴明。把這些情況都瞭解清楚了，也就知道誰勝誰敗了。孫子說："知己知彼，百戰不殆。"瞭解自己又瞭解敵人，纔能制定正確的作戰方案，這樣纔會百戰百勝。

二、攻守。孫子說："善攻者敵不知其所守，善守者敵不知其所攻。"戰爭總是有攻有守，進攻時要攻其不備，出其不意，要在敵人想不到的時間、想不到的地點發起進攻，要向敵人防守最薄弱地方或者是敵人的要害發起進攻，讓敵人跑不掉。防守時要使敵人不知道從哪裏進攻，不知道你的薄弱處在哪裏、你的要害在哪裏，讓敵人不敢追趕。三國時諸葛亮帶領蜀軍和魏軍打仗，撤退時一路走一路讓士兵們多修竈。魏軍追了幾天，看見蜀軍用來做飯的竈一天比一天多，以為蜀軍一路上到處都有伏兵，於是就不敢再追了。這在中國兵法上叫做"增竈法"。孫臏(bìn)(孫子的後代)打仗也用過這個方法，不過他用的不是"增竈法"而是"減竈法"。孫臏帶領軍隊撤退，一路走一路讓士兵們少修竈。敵人看見他們用來做飯的竈一天比一天少，以為他的士兵們每天都有不少人逃跑，於是便大膽地追了上去，結果中了孫臏的埋伏，被孫臏消滅了。

三、生死。孫子說："死地則戰。"意思是說，在戰爭中，雙方都會努力消滅敵人，保存自己。但是，有時候為了生存，必須先把自己置於死地。秦末戰爭中，韓信領兵攻打趙國。趙國的城市背後是高山，前面是大河，地形對韓信的軍隊非常不利。韓信又是新提拔的將領，威望不高。在這種

情況下，韓信帶領軍隊坐船渡過大河以後就把船燒掉了。他指揮士兵們開始進攻，敵人反攻過來，他的士兵掉頭就跑。士兵們跑到河邊時，韓信高喊："士兵們，我們已經無路可逃了，只有打敗敵人，我們纔能生存！"於是士兵們各個奮勇殺敵，打敗了趙國。這在中國兵法上叫做"置之死地而後生"。

生詞

zú	卒	die	yào hài	要害	strategic point
lùn shù	論述	expound	shǔ	蜀	Shu (*a kingdom of the three kingdoms*)
shí yè	實業	industry; practice	chè tuì	撤退	retreat; withdraw
tǒngshuài	統帥	commander	zào	竈	kitchen stove
jì lǜ	紀律	discipline	bǎo cún	保存	save; preserve
yán míng	嚴明	strict	tí bá	提拔	promote
dài	殆	danger	wēi wàng	威望	prestige
zuò zhàn	作戰	fight	dù	渡	cross; go across
fāng àn	方案	plan	zhǐ huī	指揮	command; conduct
fángshǒu	防守	defend	fèn yǒng	奮勇	courageously; bravely

聽寫

論述　保存　統帥　指揮　防守　嚴明　作戰　渡

奮勇　紀律　*撤退　威望

比一比

存 { 保存 / 生存 }　　嚴 { 嚴明 / 嚴肅 }　　帥 { 統帥 / 帥哥 }　　揮 { 指揮 / 發揮 }

練 { 訓練 / 練習 }　　方 { 方案 / 方面 }　　律 { 紀律 / 格律 }　　渡（渡河）/ 度（溫度）

詞語運用

保存

這件東西很重要，你一定要把它保存好。

提拔

他是新提拔的軍官。

這位新提拔的經理只有27歲。

威望

韓信是新提拔的將軍，威望不高。

林肯是美國最有威望的總統之一。

要害

解決問題要抓住要害。

近義詞

卒——死　　　　　作戰——打仗

根據課文回答問題

1. 《孫子兵法》一書是誰寫的？

2. 請解釋《孫子兵法》中的："知己知彼，百戰不殆"。

3. 選做題：你怎麼理解"攻其不備，出其不意"？能不能舉例說明？

孫子簡介

孫子名武，齊國人，春秋時期的軍事家。他寫的《孫子兵法》是中國古代著名的兵書，也是世界上現存最早的軍事著作。《孫子兵法》分為13篇，共6000多字，在中國軍事史上佔有重要地位，在世界軍事史上也享有極高聲譽，已被翻譯成英文、法文等多種文字。

孫武演兵

孫武精通兵法，一次去求見吳王闔閭。吳王說："你寫的《孫子兵法》我看過了，寫得非常好。你能當場為我表演一下嗎？"孫武說："可以。"吳王問："可以用婦女操練演示嗎？"孫武說："可以。"於是吳王從宮中挑選了一百八十名美女供孫武演練。孫武把她們分成兩隊，讓吳王的兩個妃子當隊長，讓宮女們拿著長矛站好。孫武把號令講了幾遍，問："聽明白了嗎？"宮女們齊聲答應："明白。"說完，孫武擊鼓發

孫子演兵圖

 中國古代哲學

出命令，可宮女們全都站在原地嬉笑，沒有人聽從他的命令。孫武說："這一次沒做好，是我沒把軍法號令講清楚，這是我做將領的過錯。"於是，他把規定又講了幾遍，然後再次擊鼓下令，宮女們仍然嬉笑不動。孫武嚴肅地說："號令講得不明白，軍法講得不清楚，是將領的錯；如果這些都講清楚了，士兵們還不按規定做，那就是隊長的過錯了。"說著就要將左右兩隊的隊長斬首。吳王急了，連忙對孫武說："我已經知道您善於用兵了。這兩個女子，您就給我留下來吧！"孫武說："我已經接受命令當您的將軍，將軍在軍隊裏可以不接受君王的命令。"說完，硬是把兩個妃子斬了。大家見孫武軍紀這麼嚴明，再也不敢胡鬧了。

後來，吳王闔閭任命孫武為吳國的大將(shuài)。他率軍打敗了強大的楚國，使吳王闔閭成為一代霸主。

生詞

shēng yù 聲譽	reputation; fame		jiàng lǐng 將領	general; military commander
hé lú 闔閭	He Lü (name)		yán sù 嚴肅	serious; grave
yǎn shì 演示	demonstrate		zhǎn shǒu 斬首	behead; cut one's head
fēi zi 妃子	concubine		hú nào 胡鬧	play the fool; make trouble
xī xiào 嬉笑	play and laugh		bà zhǔ 霸主	overlord

Lesson Seven

Sun Zi's Ideas

Sun Zi (a contemporary of Confucius; his date of birth and death are indeterminate) was a great military strategist in ancient China. He wrote a book entitled The Art of War, which systematically expounds on the different issues in war. The book has such great influence in the world that even today, many politicians, military strategists, and industrialists are still studying it. The main content of the book is discussed below.

Firstly, the book talked about the concept of "the enemy and ourselves." Any war is conducted between the enemy and our forces, so the most important task before the battle is to clearly understand the situations of the enemy and ourselves. This includes considering factors like which side is righteous, and which side is not; whose commander is better at fighting wars; who enjoys geographical advantages; whose soldiers are better trained; and whose discipline is stricter. If one has a clear understanding of all these factors and circumstances, it would be possible to predict who will be the winner or loser. As Sun Zi puts it, "Know the enemy and yourself, and in a hundred battles, you will never be in peril." This means that it is only after one has clearly understood both the enemy and himself when he can start to make appropriate military plans, and it is only then he can win every battle.

Secondly, another principle the book brought up was the idea of "attack and defense." Sun Zi said, "The general is skillful in attacking if his opponent does not know what to defend, and he is skillful in defense if his opponent does not know what to attack." War always involves attack and defense. When attacking, one must strike when the enemy is not prepared or when they least expect it. One must attack them in an unexpected time and place. The attack must target the enemy's weakest defense points or at their most strategic places, so that the enemy is unable to escape. When in defense, one must not allow the enemy to know where they can attack, or where their weak points and strategic places are, so that the enemy would not dare to pursue if they should retreat their troops. There are two good examples to illustrate this tactic. During the Three Kingdoms era, Zhuge Liang, when leading the Shu troops to fight against the Wei troops, asked his soldiers to build stoves along the way of their retreat. After pursuing them for several days, the Wei troops saw that the cooking stoves were increasing in numbers and suspected that there must be soldiers in ambush, so they gave up chasing the Shu troops. This tactic became known as "the strategy of building more stoves." Another example tells of how Sun Bin (the descendant of Sun Zi) employed the same strategy but instead of building more stoves, his method involved building fewer stoves. As he led his soldiers in retreat, Sun Bin ordered his soldiers to build fewer stoves along the way. When the enemy saw that the number of cooking stoves had become fewer, they thought that there must be many soldiers escaping each day, so they pursued fearlessly. But they were eventually ambushed by Sun Bin's troops and completely destroyed.

Thirdly, Sun Zi raised another theory in his book about the idea of "life and death." Sun Zi once said, "Place your army in deadly peril, and it will survive." In any war, both sides will try their best to destroy the enemy and preserve oneself. But sometimes, in order to survive, one must put themselves in a desperate situation first. In a battle that took place at the end of the Qin Dynasty, Han Xin led his soldiers to attack the state of Zhao. The battlefield did not favor Han Xin's army geographically at all. There were high mountains in the back and big rivers in front. Han Xin, a newly-promoted general, did not enjoy high prestige either. Taking into consideration these conditions, Han Xin nevertheless led his troops to cross the river and then burned the ship that had brought them across. When the battle began, Han Xin commanded the soldiers to attack, but the soldiers tried to run away instead when the enemy counterattacked. When the soldiers ran to the riverside, Han Xin shouted, "Soldiers, we have no way out. It is only by defeating the enemy that we can survive!" Left with no choice, the soldiers fought bravely and managed to defeat the state of Zhao. In Chinese military art, this strategy is known as "place your army in deadly peril and it will survive."

A Brief Introduction to Sun Zi

Sun Zi, who was named Sun Wu, was a citizen of the state of Qi and a military strategist in the Spring and Autumn Period. His book entitled *The Art of War* is a famous Chinese classic on military art in ancient China and is also the earliest existing military book in the world. Divided into 13 chapters and comprising more than 6,000 words, this book occupies an important place in Chinese military history and enjoys great fame in world military history. It has already been translated into many foreign languages such as English and French.

Sun Wu Demonstrates Military Art

Sun Wu was known to be a master of military art. He once went to visit He Lü, the King of Wu. The King said, "I have read your book The Art of War and it is very well-written. Can you do a demonstration on the spot for me?" "Sure," Sun Wu replied. The King asked, "Can women act as soldiers for this demonstration?" "Yes," Sun Wu agreed. The King of Wu then selected 180 beauties from the palace to aid Sun Wu in his demonstration. First, Sun Wu divided the women into two groups. He then assigned the King's two concubines to be the leader of each group, and got the women to hold long shears and stand straight. Then Sun Wu repeated the orders several times and asked the women, "Do you understand?" "Yes," answered all the women in unison. After that, Sun Wu beat the drum for them to carry out the orders, but none of the women obeyed and they continued to stand at their original places, laughing and playing. Seeing this, Sun Wu said, "We did not do well this time because I didn't explain the military orders clearly; this is my fault as a commander." So he repeated the rules several times more, then beat the drum to indicate that his orders be carried out again. But the women still remained at the original spot, and continued to laugh and play. Su Wu said gravely, "If the directions are not clear and the military orders are not explicit, it is the commander's fault; but if all of these have been clearly explained and the soldiers still refuse to obey the rules, then it is the group leader's fault."

After saying these words, Sun Wu ordered that the two leaders be beheaded. The King panicked upon hearing this, and hurriedly said, "I know now that you are very good at commanding soldiers. Please preserve these two ladies for me." But Su Wu answered, "I have accepted your order to be your commander. A commander in the army may have the right to refuse the King's order." After saying this, he kept his order and beheaded the King's two concubines. When everyone saw this, they realized how strict Sun Wu was in military discipline and dared not to create trouble anymore.

Later on, He Lü, the King of Wu, appointed Sun Wu as his commander-in-chief. Sun Wu led the armies and defeated the powerful state of Chu, making He Lü the most powerful overlord of that time.

第八課

《易經》的思想

（選讀課）

《易經》是儒家的主要經典之一。"易"有三層意思。第一層意思是變化，這部書是講變化的。第二層意思是簡明，它用符號表示不同的事物和事物的變化。它用的符號只有兩個，一個是"—"，叫做"陽"，代表天、太陽、光明、剛強、積極、運動、溫暖的力量；一個是"--"，叫做"陰"，代表地、月亮、黑暗、柔弱、消極、靜止、寒冷的力量。把這兩個符號三個一組排列起來可以得到八組符號，這八組符號叫做"八卦"，它們是：乾(qián)、坤(kūn)、坎(kǎn)、離、艮(gèn)、兌(duì)、巽(xùn)、震，分別代表天、地、水、火、山、澤、風、雷八種事物。再把這八組符號兩個一組排列起來又可以得到六十四組符號，叫做"六十四卦"，代表事物之間的不同關係和變化。第三層

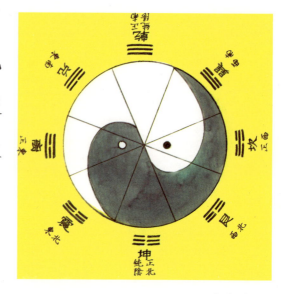

王金泰 畫

意思是不變。書的作者認為他所說的這些變化的規律是不可改變的。書中有一些文字，叫做"卦辭"和"爻辭"（yáo），是用來說明這些符號的。後來又有人寫了十篇文章，對《易經》進行解釋，叫做《易傳》。《易經》是用來算卦的書，《易傳》基本上是講哲學和倫理的。兩部書合起來叫做《周易》。

一、"一陰一陽之謂道"。《周易》認為事物都在不斷地運動變化，變化的總規律是陰陽兩種對立的力量往返交替。比如，太陽落了，月亮會昇起來；月亮落了，太陽會昇起來；太陽和月亮交替出現就有了光明。冷天過去了，熱天就來了；熱天過去了，冷天又來了；冷天和熱天往返交替就有了歲月。任何事物都是一陰一陽的往返交替，沒有一陰一陽的交替就沒有運動變化，沒有運動變化就沒有了生命。事物的存在需要有陰陽兩個方面，事物的發展變化也需要有陰陽兩個方面，在這兩個方面中陽的作用更重要，因為它代表著積極主動。但是只有陽也不行，陽需要有陰的配合纔能生成萬物並使萬物發展變化。比如，有天有地纔能有萬物，有男有女纔能有人類。陰陽兩種力量相互作用，相互交替，相反相成，這就叫做"一陰一陽之謂道"。

二、"亢龍有悔"。"亢龍"比喻地位極高而又驕傲自滿的皇帝，"有悔"就是遭到失敗。一個地位極高的人如果驕傲自滿，只知進不知退，只知安不知危，那是遲早要失敗的。事物都有陰和陽兩個方面，在這兩個方面中，陽雖然起主要作用，但是陽的力量也不能過於強大，陽的勢力過大了，就會破壞事物之間的平衡。一個國家有君和民兩個方面，在這兩個方面中，君的地位高、權力大，但是，如果他看不起人民，不尊重人民，那就會被人民趕下臺。所以我們無論是做事還是做人，都需要把握好尺度，都需要不驕不躁、謙虛謹慎。

三、"自強不息"。《周易》告訴我們，一個物只有不斷地發展變化纔能存在，一個人只有不斷地進步纔能生存。要想進步就要不斷地提高自己的道德品質，不斷地學習新的知識，不斷地增強自己的才幹；要想進步就要不怕困難，勇往直前。

王金泰 畫

生詞

jīng diǎn 經典	classics	zhǔ dòng 主動	initiative
fú hào 符號	symbol	kàng 亢	overbearing
jī jí 積極	active	shì lì 勢力	power; influence
xiāo jí 消極	passive	pínghéng 平衡	balance
suàn guà 算卦	practice divination; fortune-telling	quán lì 權力	power; authority
		chǐ dù 尺度	yardstick; scale
lún lǐ 倫理	ethics	bù jiāo bú zào 不驕不躁	free from conceit and impatience; neither arrogant nor hot-tempered
wǎng fǎn 往返	travel to and fro		
jiāo tì 交替	alternately; in turn	qiān xū 謙虛	modest
fāngmiàn 方面	aspect	jǐn shèn 謹慎	cautious; prudent
zuò yòng 作用	take the effect; function	zì qiáng bù xī 自強不息	strive constantly to improve oneself

聽寫

符號　積極　方面　權力　交替　不驕不躁　謙虛

往返　平衡　主動　*消極　謹慎

比一比

經 { 經典 / 經驗　　勢 { 勢力 / 地勢　　極 { 積極 / 北極　　虛 { 謙虛 / 虛偽

動 { 主動 / 運動 / 動機　　返 { 往返 / 返回　　謙 { 謙虛 / 謙讓　　替 { 交替 / 代替

詞語運用

積極

上哲學課時，張華總是積極發言。

姐姐愛唱歌，每次表演她都積極參加。

主動

弟弟從不主動練琴，總要媽媽催。

哥哥主動提出要學中文。

近義詞

往返——來回　　　　　　才幹——才能——能力

反義詞

光明——黑暗　　積極——消極　　陰——陽

運動——靜止　　驕傲——謙虛

根據課文回答問題

1. 什麼是《易經》、《易傳》、《周易》？

2. "易"的三層意思都是什麼？

3. 什麼是"八卦"？

4. 請解釋《周易》中講的"一陰一陽之謂道"。

5. 請解釋《周易》中的"自強不息"。

詞語解釋

勇往直前——勇敢地一直往前走。

自強不息——努力向上，永遠不放鬆自己。

驕傲自滿——滿足於自己已有的成績，自以為了不起，看不起別人。

相配詞語連線

遭到　　　　才幹

破壞　　　　尺度

增強　　　　平衡

把握　　　　失敗

English Translation

Lesson Eight

Yi Jing's Ideas

(An Optional Lesson)

Yi Jing (the Book of Changes) is one of the main Confucian classics. The word "yi" has three meanings. The first meaning is transformation, and this is what the book discusses. The second meaning is simplicity because the book uses only two symbols to express different things and changes. One symbol is "⚊." Known as "yang," it symbolizes the power of heaven, the sun, brightness, hardness, activity, motion, and warmth. The other symbol is "⚋," which is known as "yin," and this symbolizes the power of the earth, moon, darkness, weakness, passivity, stillness, and coldness. Combining these two symbols in a trigram will result in eight combinations which are known as the "Eight Trigrams (ba gua)": qian, kun, kan, li, gen, dui, xun, and zhen, symbolizing heaven, earth, water, fire, mountain, marsh, wind, and thunder respectively. By combining any two of these trigrams with one another, a total of 64 combinations can be obtained. Known as the "64 Hexagrams (liu shi si gua)," it expresses the different relations and changes among things. The third meaning of "yi" is invariability. In the author's opinion, all the laws of changes mentioned are invariable. There are some textual comments in the book called "gua ci" and "yao ci," which are used to explain the symbols. After that, 10 articles were written to explain the implications of Yi Jing and this eventually became known as Yi Zhuan. Yi Jing was used for fortune-telling while Yi Zhuan basically talks about philosophy and ethics. The combination of these two books makes Zhou Yi. The main principles of Zhou Yi are discussed be-

low.

Firstly, one of the main principles is that of "one *yang* and one *yin* makes *Tao*." Zhou Yi raises the idea that all things are constantly moving and changing, and the general law of change is that these two opposite powers, *yin* and *yang*, are changing alternately. For example, the moon will rise after the sun sets and likewise, the sun will rise after the moon sets. The alternate appearance of the sun and the moon brings brightness. After the cold weather comes the hot, and after the hot weather comes the cold. The alternating change between the hot and cold weather forms the seasons. Everything alternates between *yin* and *yang*, without which there will be no movement and change. Without movement and change, there will be no life. Thus, both the existence of things and their changes require the two aspects of *yin* and *yang*. Comparatively speaking, *yang* has a more important function because it represents being active and taking initiative. But having *yang* alone will not suffice because it is only when yang and yin are combined when everything can come into being and develop and change. For instance, all things come into existence only after heaven and earth come into being, and human beings come into being only after men and women are joined. The powers of *yin* and *yang* interact, alternate and complement each other—this is called "one *yang* and one *yin* makes *Tao*."

Secondly, another concept *Zhou Yi* discussed is about how "the overbearing dragon will have cause to repent (*kang long you hui*)." The term "*kang long*" refers to a conceited emperor who has high social status, while "*you hui*" means to meet with defeat. A person who is conceited and has a high status will be doomed to failure if he only knows how to march forward instead of retreating and never considers danger in times of peace. The reason for this is that everything has two aspects: *yin* and *yang*. Although *yang* plays a main role, the balance between things will be destroyed if *yang* becomes too powerful. This is especially true with a nation. A nation is composed of the king and his people. Comparatively, the king is in a higher status and has more power. However, if he despises and disrespects his people, he will eventually be overthrown by them. Therefore, whether we are learning how to do things or how to behave like a virtuous person, we need to have a good yardstick, and learn to be free from conceit and impatience, being modest and prudent.

Thirdly, the book also talks about how one should "strive constantly to improve oneself." *Zhou Yi* tells us that something can exist only if it develops and changes constantly. Similarly, a person can survive only if he makes sustained progress. Making progress calls for continual improvement of one's moralities, constant acquiring of new knowledge, and perpetually enhancing one's abilities. In order to

生字表（繁）

1. 臘(là) 儒(rú) 釋(shì) 割(gē) 忠(zhōng) 恕(shù) 施(shī) 遵(zūn) 穩(wěn) 秩(zhì)
2. 惻(cè) 謙(qiān) 義(yì) 栽(zāi) 培(péi)
3. 荀(xún) 聯(lián) 禦(yù) 鋒(fēng) 社(shè)
4. 討(tǎo) 享(xiǎng) 兼(jiān) 效(xiào)
5. 醜(chǒu) 檐(yán)
6. 霜(shuāng) 耍(shuǎ) 擾(rǎo) 脊(jǐ)
7. 卒(zú) 述(shù) 殆(dài) 案(àn) 蜀(shǔ) 撤(chè) 竈(zào) 渡(dù)
8. 符(fú) 卦(guà) 亢(kàng) 權(quán) 躁(zào) 謹(jǐn) 慎(shèn)

共計45個生字

生字表（简）

	là	rú	shì	gē	zhōng	shù	shī	zūn	wěn	zhì
1.	腊	儒	释	割	忠	恕	施	遵	稳	秩

	cè	qiān	yì	zāi	péi
2.	恻	谦	义	栽	培

	xún	lián	yù	fēng	shè
3.	荀	联	御	锋	社

	tǎo	xiǎng	jiān	xiào
4.	讨	享	兼	效

	chǒu	yán
5.	丑	檐

	shuāng	shuǎ	rǎo	jǐ
6.	霜	耍	扰	脊

	zú	shù	dài	àn	shǔ	chè	zào	dù
7.	卒	述	殆	案	蜀	撤	灶	渡

	fú	guà	kàng	quán	zào	jǐn	shèn
8.	符	卦	亢	权	躁	谨	慎

共计45个生字

生詞表（繁）

1. 教育 (jiào yù)　希臘 (xī là)　儒家 (rú jiā)　學派 (xué pài)　道德 (dào dé)　高尚 (gāo shàng)　解釋 (jiě shì)　感情 (gǎn qíng)
   精神境界 (jīng shén jìng jiè)　割斷 (gē duàn)　忠恕 (zhōng shù)　寬容 (kuān róng)　施 (shī)　事業 (shì yè)　克制 (kè zhì)　約束 (yuē shù)
   行為 (xíng wéi)　遵守 (zūn shǒu)　規範 (guī fàn)　穩定 (wěn dìng)　秩序 (zhì xù)

2. 理論 (lǐ lùn)　惻隱 (cè yǐn)　同情 (tóng qíng)　羞恥 (xiū chǐ)　謙讓 (qiān ràng)　善惡 (shàn è)　區別 (qū bié)　正義 (zhèng yì)
   順利 (shùn lì)　對待 (duì dài)　栽 (zāi)　培養 (péi yǎng)　根本 (gēn běn)　領導 (lǐng dǎo)　人民 (rén mín)　擁護 (yōng hù)　愛戴 (ài dài)
   資格 (zī gé)

3. 荀子 (xún zǐ)　偽 (wěi)　具有 (jù yǒu)　制度 (zhì dù)　性質 (xìng zhì)　功能 (gōng néng)　規律 (guī lǜ)　目的 (mù dì)　聯繫 (lián xì)
   依靠 (yī kào)　改造 (gǎi zào)　禦寒 (yù hán)　鋒利 (fēng lì)　組織 (zǔ zhī)　社會 (shè huì)　集體 (jí tǐ)　發揮 (fā huī)　企圖 (qǐ tú)

4. 成果 (chéng guǒ)　討論 (tǎo lùn)　飲料 (yǐn liào)　生存 (shēng cún)　佔有 (zhàn yǒu)　享受 (xiǎng shòu)　兼 (jiān)　爭奪 (zhēng duó)
   互利 (hù lì)　動機 (dòng jī)　效果 (xiào guǒ)　體現 (tǐ xiàn)　主張 (zhǔ zhāng)

5. 充分 (chōng fèn)　圍繞 (wéi rào)　理解 (lǐ jiě)　法則 (fǎ zé)　對立面 (duì lì miàn)　前提 (qián tí)　醜 (chǒu)　堅硬 (jiān yìng)
   柔軟 (róu ruǎn)　屋檐 (wū yán)　剛強 (gāng qiáng)　保持 (bǎo chí)　奪取 (duó qǔ)　一旦 (yí dàn)　具體 (jù tǐ)　外交 (wài jiāo)
   內務 (nèi wù)

6. 代表 (dài biǎo)　地位 (dì wèi)　整個 (zhěng gè)　一切 (yí qiè)　特徵 (tè zhēng)　存在 (cún zài)　功用 (gōng yòng)　霜 (shuāng)
   戲耍 (xì shuǎ)　訓練 (xùn liàn)　截短 (jié duǎn)　順應 (shùn yìng)　打擾 (dǎ rǎo)　脊背 (jǐ bèi)　憑借 (píng jiè)　條件 (tiáo jiàn)
   融入 (róng rù)

7. 卒 論述 實業 統帥 紀律 嚴明 殆 作戰
   方案 防守 要害 蜀 撤退 竈 保存 提拔
   威望 渡 指揮 奮勇

8. 經典 符號 積極 消極 算卦 倫理 往返 交替
   方面 作用 主動 亢 勢力 平衡 權力 尺度
   不驕不躁 謙虛 謹慎 自強不息

共計144個生詞

生词表（简）

1. 教育 jiào yù　希腊 xī là　儒家 rú jiā　学派 xué pài　道德 dào dé　高尚 gāo shàng　解释 jiě shì　感情 gǎn qíng
   精神境界 jīng shén jìng jiè　割断 gē duàn　忠恕 zhōng shù　宽容 kuān róng　施 shī　事业 shì yè　克制 kè zhì　约束 yuē shù
   行为 xíng wéi　遵守 zūn shǒu　规范 guī fàn　稳定 wěn dìng　秩序 zhì xù

2. 理论 lǐ lùn　恻隐 cè yǐn　同情 tóng qíng　羞耻 xiū chǐ　谦让 qiān ràng　善恶 shàn è　区别 qū bié　正义 zhèng yì
   顺利 shùn lì　对待 duì dài　栽 zāi　培养 péi yǎng　根本 gēn běn　领导 lǐng dǎo　人民 rén mín　拥护 yōng hù　爱戴 ài dài
   资格 zī gé

3. 荀子 xún zǐ　伪 wěi　具有 jù yǒu　制度 zhì dù　性质 xìng zhì　功能 gōng néng　规律 guī lǜ　目的 mù dì　联系 lián xì
   依靠 yī kào　改造 gǎi zào　御寒 yù hán　锋利 fēng lì　组织 zǔ zhī　社会 shè huì　集体 jí tǐ　发挥 fā huī　企图 qǐ tú

4. 成果 chéng guǒ　讨论 tǎo lùn　饮料 yǐn liào　生存 shēng cún　占有 zhàn yǒu　享受 xiǎng shòu　兼 jiān　争夺 zhēng duó
   互利 hù lì　动机 dòng jī　效果 xiào guǒ　体现 tǐ xiàn　主张 zhǔ zhāng

5. 充分 chōng fèn　围绕 wéi rào　理解 lǐ jiě　法则 fǎ zé　对立面 duì lì miàn　前提 qián tí　丑 chǒu　坚硬 jiān yìng
   柔软 róu ruǎn　屋檐 wū yán　刚强 gāng qiáng　保持 bǎo chí　夺取 duó qǔ　一旦 yí dàn　具体 jù tǐ　外交 wài jiāo
   内务 nèi wù

6. 代表 dài biǎo　地位 dì wèi　整个 zhěng gè　一切 yí qiè　特征 tè zhēng　存在 cún zài　功用 gōng yòng　霜 shuāng
   戏耍 xì shuǎ　训练 xùn liàn　截短 jié duǎn　顺应 shùn yìng　打扰 dǎ rǎo　脊背 jǐ bèi　凭借 píng jiè　条件 tiáo jiàn
   融入 róng rù

7. 卒 论述 实业 统帅 纪律 严明 殆 作战
方案 防守 要害 蜀 撤退 灶 保存 提拔
威望 渡 指挥 奋勇

8. 经典 符号 积极 消极 算卦 伦理 往返 交替
方面 作用 主动 亢 势力 平衡 权力 尺度
不骄不躁 谦虚 谨慎 自强不息

共计144个生词

第二課

一 寫生詞

惻	隱										
謙	讓										
正	義										
栽											
培	養										

二 組詞

端_____ 善_____ 擁_____ 仁_____

栽_____ 順_____ 謙_____ 基_____

羞_____ 護_____ 逐_____ 培_____

管_____ 擁_____ 義_____ 待_____

理_____ 順_____ 愛_____ 資_____

三　選字組詞

（尊　遵）守　　　（栽　載）種　　　（繼　記）承

（尊　遵）敬　　　記（栽　載）　　　（記　繼）錄

（事　是）非　　　道（得　德）　　　（歉　謙）讓

（事　是）情　　　獲（得　德）　　　道（歉　謙）

四　讀一讀，比一比

端著——端正　　　害羞——羞恥

禮貌——面貌　　　亞軍——亞聖

區別——地區　　　發展——頭髮

正義——意思　　　間斷——時間

五　填空

1. 孟子是孔子的主要＿＿＿＿人之一，被中國人尊稱為＿＿＿＿。

2. 對於人為什麼會有道德的問題，孟子提出了＿＿＿＿的理論。

六 選詞填空(請把詞語寫在空白處)

禮　　仁　　智　　義

1. 孟子認為"惻隱之心"會發展成為_____,"羞惡之心"會發展成為_____,"辭讓之心"會發展成為_____,"是非之心"會發展成為_____。

拔苗助長　　逐漸　　不間斷

2. 孟子認為人的道德品質是_____培養起來的,既要_____地努力,又不要_____。

七 造句

1. 愛護_____

2. 說明_____

3. 逐漸_____

八 詞語解釋

1. 是非——

2. 急於求成——

九 請寫一寫"拔苗助長"的故事（至少寫四句話）

十 請寫一寫孟子"仁政"的思想（至少寫五句話）

十一 熟讀課文

第四課

一 寫生詞

討	論									

享	受									

兼										

效	果									

二 組詞

討_____　　蹄_____　　獲_____　　飲_____

動_____　　佔_____　　享_____　　受_____

兼_____　　交_____　　效_____　　欺_____

張_____　　奪_____　　壯_____　　實_____

存_____　　利_____　　成_____　　德_____

三 選字組詞

主(張 章)　　(站 佔)立　　(效 校)果

文(張 章)　　(站 佔)有　　學(效 校)

(爭 掙)奪　　(培 倍)養　　討(論 輪)

(爭 掙)扎　　幾(培 倍)　　(論 輪)流

四 選擇填空(請把詞語寫在空白處)

1. 人必須通過勞動纔能有衣穿、有飯吃,纔能_____。

（存在　生存）

2. 不勞動而佔有別人的勞動_____是不道德的。

（結果　成果）

3. 以大欺小,以強欺弱,以富欺貧都是不_____的。

（道德　品質）

4. 如果人與人、國與國之間都能互相愛,世界上就沒有_____,沒有戰爭了。

（奪取　爭奪）

五 選詞填空(請把詞語寫在空白處)

重視　　手工業者　　重要　　討論　　創立

墨子是中國_____的思想家、哲學家。他_____了墨家學派。墨子和他的學生大多數是_____,他們都很_____勞動和勞動成果,經常_____勞動的問題。

六 詞語解釋

不勞而獲——

七 根據課文回答問題

1. 墨子創立的學派叫什麼?

答:_____

2. 墨子提出的"兼相愛"與孔子講的"愛人"有什麼不同?

答:_____

_____

3. 墨子提出："每一個人都應該勞動，人只有參加勞動纔能享受勞動成果，不勞而獲是不道德的。"你的看法是什麼？

答：＿＿＿＿＿＿＿＿＿＿＿＿＿＿＿＿＿＿＿＿＿

八　熟讀課文

第六課

一　寫生詞

霜	雪											

戲	耍											

打	擾											

脊	背											

二　組詞

融_____　　括_____　　忘_____　　隨_____

莊_____　　代_____　　表_____　　徵_____

整_____　　條_____　　訓_____　　脊_____

需_____　　耍_____　　憑_____　　遮_____

擾_____　　切_____　　任_____　　存_____

三 選字組詞

（代 帶）表　　（功 工）能　　戲(要 耍)

（代 帶）領　　（功 工）作　　(要 耍)求

恐(懼 具)　　打(繞 擾)

(懼 具)有　　圍(繞 擾)

四 寫出近義詞

一切——　　　　　　依靠——

五 寫出反義詞

無限——

六 選擇填空（請將詞語寫在空白處）

1. 莊子是_____學派的。（儒家　道家）

2. 自然而然，順應自然，是_____的觀點。

（儒家　道家）

3. 莊子的思想也是_____著"道"展開的。

（環繞　圍繞）

4. 如果把鶴的腿_____短了，它就不能生活了。

（截　栽）

七 造句

1. 一切_____

2. 代表_____

八 相配詞語連線

整個　　　　　地位

打敗　　　　　事物

很高的　　　　宇宙

一切　　　　　敵人

九 根據課文回答問題

莊子認為:"人應該尊重自然、順應自然,而不要按照自己的願望去改變自然、破壞自然、打擾自然。只有這樣,世界纔能更好地存在,人類纔能更好地生存。"

你是怎樣理解莊子的觀點的?

答:_____

_____

_____

_____

十 熟讀課文

第八課

一 寫生詞

符	號											
算	卦											
兀												
權	力											
謹	慎											
不	驕	不	躁									

二 組詞

倫_____   喻_____   斷_____   度_____

列_____   寒_____   明_____   暗_____

典_____   符_____   積_____   消_____

替_____   靜_____   卦_____   返_____

自強_____   不驕_____   勇往_____

三 选字组词

经（点　典）　　简（明　名）　　排（例　列）
顶（点　典）　　著（明　名）　　举（例　列）

往（反　返）　　急（燥　躁）　　（歉　谦）虚
正（反　返）　　干（燥　躁）　　道（歉　谦）

自（满　瞒）
隐（满　瞒）

四 读一读

骄傲自满　　谦虚谨慎　　勇往直前　　不骄不躁
积极主动　　往返交替　　相反相成　　自强不息

五 寫出近義詞

來回——　　　　　　　　　　　　才幹——

六 寫出反義詞

　　光明——　　　　驕傲——　　　　陰——

　　消極——　　　　運動——

七 選詞填空

　　　　　《易傳》　　《周易》　　《易經》

　　1.＿＿＿＿是儒家經典之一,是用來算卦的書。＿＿＿＿基本上是講哲學和倫理的,是對《易經》的解釋。《易經》和《易傳》兩部書合起來叫做＿＿＿＿。

　　　　　事物的變化　　規律不變　　簡明

　　2."易"有三層意思,第一層是講＿＿＿＿,第二層意思是＿＿＿＿,第三層是講＿＿＿＿。

　　3.陰的符號是＿＿＿＿;陽的符號是＿＿＿＿。

八 造句

　　積極＿＿＿＿＿＿＿＿＿＿＿＿＿＿＿＿＿＿＿＿＿＿

九 詞語解釋

1. 勇往直前——

2. 自強不息——

3. 驕傲自滿——

十 根據課文回答問題

1. 什麼是"一陰一陽之謂道"？

答：_____

_____

_____

2. 如何理解《周易》中講的"自強不息"的觀點？

答：_____

_____

_____

十一 熟讀課文

第二課聽寫

第四課聽寫

第六課聽寫

中國古代哲學

第八課聽寫

練習紙

練習紙

中國古代哲學

第一課

一　寫生詞

希臘										
儒家										
解釋										
割斷										
忠恕										
施										
遵守										
穩定										
秩序										

二　組詞

哲_____　　穩_____　　割_____　　釋_____

德_____　　品_____　　誠_____　　精_____

忠_____　　行_____　　秩_____　　遵_____

三 選字組詞

品德高(上　尚)　　發(恕　怒)　　行(為　偽)

精神(竟　境)界　　(克　刻)制　　(尊　遵)守

克(己　已)復禮　　解(譯　釋)　　(割　害)斷

四 寫出反義詞

有害——　　　　　　　真誠——

五 選擇填空(請將詞語寫在空白處)

1. 孔子是_____時期的人。(春秋　戰國)

2. 孔子創立了_____學派。(儒家　道家)

3. 孔子是個偉大的_____、_____。

(哲學家　天文學家　教育家)

六 選詞填空(請將詞語寫在空白處)

成功　感情　影響　真誠　相連

1. 孔子的思想對於中國和世界都有很大的_____。

2. 愛人要_____，而不能虛情假意。

3. 親朋好友和你最有_____。

4. 宇宙間一切東西都是血肉_____的。

5. 人都希望得到幸福、快樂和事業的_____。

七 造句

遵守_____

八 詞語解釋

1. 有益——

2. 真誠——

3. 創立——

九 請簡單解釋孔子的觀點

1. "仁"：_____

2. "忠恕之道"：_____

3. "己所不欲，勿施於人"：_____

十　根據課文回答問題

　　1. 孔子認為最根本、最高尚的品質是什麼？

　　　答：_____

　　　_____

　　2. "克己復禮"的"克己"指的是什麼？"復禮"指的是什麼？

　　　答：_____

　　　_____

　　　_____

十一　寫一寫你所知道的孔子（300字左右）

_____

_____

_____

_____

_____

十二　熟讀課文

第三課

一 寫生詞

荀	子										
聯	繫										
禦	寒										
鋒	利										
社	會										

二 組詞

性____　　慣____　　欲____　　律____

互____　　聯____　　營____　　寒____

社____　　集____　　限____　　揮____

鋒____　　益____　　功____　　靠____

改____　　織____　　具____　　目____

三 寫出近義詞

區別——　　　　　　　　打算——

四 寫出反義詞

偽——　　　　　　　　個人——

五 給多音字注漢語拼音

1. 荀子認為人性是惡的（　　）。

2. 自然界的運動變化並沒有什麼目的（　　）。

六 選擇填空（請把詞語寫在空白處）

1. 自然界的各種事物都是相互_____、相互依靠的。

（聯繫　關係）

2. 人能認識自然、利用自然、_____自然。

（改變　改造）

3. 人沒有_____的爪牙。（山峰　鋒利）

4. 人能利用_____的力量戰勝其他事物。

（集中　集體）

5. 應該分清什麼是自然界的_____和功能。

（品質　性質）

6. 荀子提出"_____"。（性惡論　性善論）

7. 孟子提出"_____"。（性惡論　性善論）

8. "明於天人之分"是_____提出的。（孔子　荀子）

七　造句

目的_____

八　相配詞語連線

制定　　　　秩序

破壞　　　　法規

戰勝　　　　教育

接受　　　　高尚

品德　　　　敵人

九　請簡單解釋荀子的"性惡論"

十　請舉例説明什麼事物是"有限"的，什麼事物是"無限"的

十一　寫一寫你所知道的荀子（300字左右）

十二　熟讀課文

第五課

一 寫生詞

醜											

屋	檐										

二 組詞

理_____　　充_____　　繞_____　　醜_____

堅_____　　軟_____　　論_____　　強_____

旦_____　　奪_____　　具_____　　甚_____

慧_____　　持_____　　任_____　　衰_____

則_____　　體_____　　提_____

三 選字組詞（畫圈）

（理　里）解　　　（剛　鋼）強　　　充（份　分）

屋（沿　檐）　　　圍（繞　澆）　　　前（題　提）

一（但　旦）　　　（揉　柔）弱

四 寫出近義詞

規律——　　　　　　　不論——

五 寫出反義詞

柔弱——　　　　　　　美——

柔軟——　　　　　　　正面——

六 選擇填空（請把詞語寫在空白處）

1. 老子的思想_____體現了中國人的_____。

（充分　充滿　才智　智慧）

2. 老子的思想是圍繞著對"道"的_____展開的。

（理論　理解）

3. 天地萬物都有它發展變化的_____。

（規定　規律）

4. 弱小的事物能夠_____強大的事物。

（戰勝　勝利）

5. 任何事物_____強大了，也就會逐漸衰落了。

（但是　一旦）

6. "無為"就是不去做任何_____的事情。

（具有　具體）

七　選詞填空（請把詞語寫在空白處）

生存　　保持　　剛強　　狀態　　無論

"柔弱勝_____"說的是_____一個人還是一個國家，要想長期_____下去，就要_____柔弱的_____。

八　造句

一旦_____

九　解釋下列老子的觀點

1. "反者道之動"

2. "柔弱勝剛強"

十　舉三個例子說明每一種事物都有自己的對立面

十一　寫一寫你所知道的老子（300字左右）

十二　熟讀課文

第七課

一 寫生詞

卒												
論述												
殆												
方案												
蜀												
撤退												
竈												
渡												

二 組詞

述____ 存____ 實____ 帥____

威____ 渡____ 勇____ 防____

訓____ 提____ 拔____ 撤____

紀____ 統____ 要____ 指____

三 選字組詞

包(括 舌)　　(做 作)戰　　作(業 葉)

統(師 帥)　　(方 防)案　　提(拔 撥)

撤(退 腿)　　(紀 記)律　　情(況 兄)

四 寫出近義詞

卒——　　　　　　　　打仗——

五 選擇填空(請把詞語寫在空白處)

1. 孫子是中國古代偉大的_____家。(哲學 軍事)

2.《孫子兵法》_____地論述了戰爭中的各種問題。

(系統 傳統)

3. 軍隊的紀律必須_____。(嚴厲 嚴明)

4. 作戰要_____敵我雙方的情況。(懂得 瞭解)

5. 戰爭中要進攻敵人的_____。(要害 厲害)

6. 戰爭中雙方都會努力_____敵人，_____自己。

(消失 消滅 保存 保持)

六 選詞填空（請把詞語寫在空白處）

威望　　生存　　帶領　　不利

1. 趙國城市的地形對韓信的軍隊非常_____。

2. 韓信是新提拔的將領，_____不高。

3. 韓信_____軍隊坐船渡過大河後就把船燒掉了。

4. 我們無路可逃，只有打敗敵人，我們纔能_____。

七 造句

1. 瞭解_____

2. 保存_____

八 相配詞語連線

打敗　　　　　　情況

瞭解　　　　　　軍隊

制定　　　　　　敵人

指揮　　　　　　方案

九　根據課文回答問題

《孫子兵法》一書是誰寫的，在什麼時代寫的？
答：_____
_____

十　請解釋孫子"知己知彼，百戰不殆"的觀點

_____
_____

十一　熟讀課文

第一課聽寫

第三課聽寫

第五課聽寫

第七課聽寫

練習紙

中國古代哲學

練習紙

中國古代哲學